Advance Praise for Curing the Unmet Needs Disease: Financial Advisor Edition

"Reading the book seemed as though everything I was thinking was right there in front of me. Curing The Unmet Needs Disease allowed me drill down into looking at myself and discover my "unmet needs" which allowed me to look at my business in a different light and live a much bigger vision."

Steven Bakouris
Freedom 55 Financial
Regina, SK

"Curing The Unmet Needs Disease gave me the tools to become more clear and confident enabling me to steer my business in the right direction."

Edna Keep
Assante Financial Management
Regina, SK

i

"Finally, someone has gone beyond the mechanics of success, pulled back the curtain, and allowed us to really understand what holds us back from realizing our goals. Simon Reilly has pulled together his insights to help anyone identify and release their self-limiting, self-sabotaging beliefs which are driven by their "Unmet Needs" so that they can reach the levels of success they dream of."

Michael Beck
The Insurance & Advisor Coach
Bend, OR

"This book is a very easy read and has brought me new insight and commitment to my business. It has helped me identify my unmet needs that are holding me back from expressing and living my values."

Graham Calder, CFP, CLU, CH. F. C., RHU
Director, Business Development
Freedom 55 Financial
Nanaimo, BC

"Simon's book is an excellent summation of his program. It provides an awakening, practical transition for advisors from surviving a demanding career to becoming an encouraging, enlightened educator. Simon's guidance has injected my career and personal life with awareness, composure and optimism. I provide the commitment to a better life, he provides the stepping stones."

Mark A. Berkin, BSc, CSA
Account Executive
Worldsource Financial Management Inc.
Waterloo, ON

"I wouldn't have lasted in this business without Simon's coaching and support. I still struggle at times with the "unmet needs disease". This book provides the insight, understanding and systems to assist in ending the struggle."

Glennis Deslippe BSN, RHU
Account Manager
Group Benefits
Integral Financial Services Inc.
Surrey, BC

"This book is a roadmap for success for the 21st Century advisor. Simon's message will help every Advisor sharpen their saw".

Stuart Crawford, CLU
Director of Sales, Ontario
Industrial Alliance, Life Insurance and Financial Services
Toronto, ON

"I was very intrigued by how you identified the reader's challenges, and did not make them feel wrong for it. I really believe that you have a winner here. Your book will be difficult to put down once one starts to read it. Today I practice the principles that Simon taught me ten years ago!"

Nelson F Deslippe, CFP, CLU, ChFC
Integral Financial Services Inc.
Surrey, BC

"I found the book to be good in two ways. The book provides a very practical scorecard to self evaluate yourself and your business. Secondly, it is very orderly as it takes you through the steps allowing you to see where the roadblocks (and then fix them) are to the issues of growth in any part of life."

Donald A. Daggett. B.Sc., CIMA.
Associate Investment Advisor
CIBC Wood Gundy
Waterloo, Ont.

"Everyone today is busy but are we busy at the things we should be focusing on. This book is a great read, full of clarity and beneficial to anyone who wants to move their practice up a notch!"

Diane Dupuis, CLU, CHFC, CFP
Dupuis Langen Financial Management (1985) Ltd.
Richmond, BC

"During fifteen years of covering advisor issues, I have seen many of the roadblocks to success that Simon Reilly crystallizes in his text. He neither over-emphasizes nor minimizes their importance but offers solutions for the advisor's consideration."

Al Emid
Senior Journalist
The Insurance Journal
Toronto Bureau

"Simon Reilly brings with him not only a wealth of experience but very unique insight into the ways in which advisors and their clients think. He made me realize my full potential as a manager in the financial planning industry."

Rohini Kapoor
Desjardins Financial Services
Victoria, BC

"This book is a must read for every advisor who is interested in building a successful business based on their core values."

Paul Ghezzi, CA
Founder
DBS Private Client Group Inc.
Markham, ON

"Without Simon Reilly's unique insights I doubt that I would have been able to get out of the cage I was in for over 30 years. I finally understood what was holding me back, and how to get the problem out of the way. You really need this book."

Paul Lauzon CFP, CLU, CHFC, EPC
Lauzon Financial Advisors Inc.
Kelowna, BC

"If you want to be a successful financial advisor, you have to do what successful advisors do – get rid of the beliefs which are holding you back. "Curing The Unmet Needs Disease" will get you moving on the right path to your successful future."

Robert Gignac
Author - Rich is a State of Mind
Blonay, Switzerland

"Simon Reilly's book of practical business advice is readable and inspirational. I like his use of anecdotes and analogies in making concepts clear."

Terry McBride CLU, CFP
NCSAS Advocis Secretary
Raymond James Ltd.
Saskatoon, SK

"Providing software to advisors also exposes us to both leading advisors and the laggards. Simon boldly talks to the latter in this book and shares great insight that can help them evolve their business. He helps advisors isolate their own unmet needs and put a practical plan into action. This is definitely required reading for any advisor who wants to gain more satisfaction from all those hours you invest in your working life."

Jim Graddon
GM, Canadian Operations
E-Z Data, Ulc.
Oakville, ON

"Simon's system takes you to the root of the issues. That way he treats the cause of the problem, and not the symptoms."

Grant McPhail
Rice Financial Group
Brandon, MB

"Simon really understands financial advisors at a deep level. Curing The Unmet Needs Disease helped me to improve my focus, work on my business versus in my business, delegate more and implement systems to improve customer service."

Beatrice Hale, CMA BA CFP CFSB CSA FMA CIM FCSI
Manulife Securities Inc.
Manulife Securities Insurance Inc.
Whitby, ON

"The content is excellent. This will certainly cause advisors to think about a significantly bigger picture. Eliminate your unmet needs and you win the game of life."

Duncan Robinson
Freedom 55 Financial
Surrey, BC

"This easy read helped me realize I was supplying the mortar for the very walls that held me back. Thankyou Simon for providing tools and techniques in a book that so aptly describes me. I'm awake now and the future is incredibly bright and exciting!"

Barb Holland
Executive Director
The Holland Benefits Group
Windsor, ON

"The only lasting changes a person can make are from the inside out. Simon is not only one of the best in the business at understanding this, but a specialist at implementing it. Curing The Unmet Needs Disease goes bone deep, I'd recommend this book to anyone looking to be the best they can be."

Richard Savage
Sr. Vice President & Director
Blackmont Capital
Vancouver, BC

"Curing The Unmet Needs Disease will help you to become a better financial advisor and is the missing link to building a profitable and sustainable financial advisor business."

Tom Miller, President
Alex Nicholson, VP Education
Pro-Seminars
Beamsville, ON

"Simon understands the everyday challenges that are faced by most financial advisors. Curing The Unmet Needs Disease offers solutions that work and help you grow to your full potential."

Bill Schmidt
Investors Group
Calgary, AB

"Originally I thought 'just another motivational book' but I started reading and found it flowed so easily and hit home with extremely interesting thoughts. It made me think about my own unmet needs and values. It is inspirational. It read just like you were standing there speaking and challenging me."

Doug Vanderburgh, President
Queensbury Insurance Brokers Inc.
Hagersville, ON

Curing the Unmet Needs Disease:

How to prosper in business
by meeting your unmet needs.

Financial Advisor Edition

By Simon Reilly

BUSINESS BUILDING books Share your knowledge.

First Edition

ISBN: 978-1-934509-23-4

Library of Congress Control Number: 2008939292

Printed in the Canada.

First printing: 2008

Cover illustration by:
    Cyanotype.ca

Published by:
    Business Building Books
    1301 Colby Drive
    Saint Peters, Missouri 63376
    FemmeOsagePublishing.com

Contents

Dedication

This work is dedicated to my mother Irene Reilly and to the memory of my father John Reilly. Irene and John immigrated to Canada in 1957 to provide me with a better life.

My parents gave me the gifts of a strong soul, heart, body and mind along with the commitment, courage, dedication, perseverance and strong work ethic to understand both the areas of strength and the areas to strengthen.

Acknowledgements

Thank you to my loving wife and business partner, Laura Reilly, the happiest and most grounded person that I know. Without your help, this book would not be possible.

Thank you to my friend Pat Finucane, my understanding sounding board since he first heard the idea for this book seven years ago.

Many thanks go out to Debra Silverman, who introduced me to my own unique behavioral style and the unique behavioral styles of others. To Tony Robbins, who introduced me to professional personal development, to Duane O'Kane and Sandy Levey, who first taught me how to clear my negative emotions and negative beliefs. Thanks to Coach U and the late Thomas Leonard, who first introduced me to *Unmet Needs*, and to Target Training International who introduced me to the science of values and behaviors assessments.

Thank you to Chris Barrow, who helped me to regain my voice at a time my business was floundering and to Kim Black, for her continued IT ideas and support. Appreciation goes out to Christina Greenway and Amada Nicholas who support us as Virtual Assistants providing us with an enormous amount of expertise in many different areas. Thank you to Simon Parsons for keeping all of our computer systems running both in the office and on the road.

Gratitude goes out to Bill Bishop for your help to refine our packaging and for the fine tuning of the title of this book.

Thank you to Lynne Klippel, my publishing project manager, for your tough love and for sending me back to the drawing board more than once.

I am grateful for the patience and understanding of my developmental editor Linda Dessau, who crafted an enormous amount of writing into a message that I believe is the missing link to help masses of people clear the way to their unrealized dreams. Thank you to Justin DiPego for copy editing the last version of the book.

And thank you to all of my clients from over the past two decades, who have faced their greatest fears and gone on to add value to themselves, their family and all whom they serve.

Who is Leading Advisor?

Leading Advisor is Simon Reilly (Coach), and Laura Reilly (Operations Manager). They are values and behavioral analysts and they work exclusively with the financial advisor industry.

Simon received personal and business coaching training from Robbins Research International from 1990–1993 and Coach U from 1995–1999 and values and behavioral analysis training from Target Training International in 1997. He continues to develop and enhance his training, combining business and personal development with attitudinal healing, emotional intelligence, emotional release work, family systems theory, and inner child work.

At the time of this writing, Simon has 26,000 hours of one-on-one coaching experience. He is a sought after speaker for associations and companies such as Advocis, Canada Life, Financial Management (BC) Inc, IDC Financial, London Life/Freedom 55, Pro-Seminars, The

Cooperators, The Cumis Group and The Independent Financial Brokers Association. He has spoken to nearly 10,000 advisors across the country, from Nanaimo, BC to Saint Johns, NB. He was profiled in The Insurance Journal and has been published in The Advocis FORUM Magazine. His monthly column appears in the online magazine, Advisor.ca.

Laura gained her management and operations expertise in the hospitality industry with The Shangri-la Group. While working within a large hotel, she quickly determined that each department runs as an independent business. Her experience ranges through areas of finance, hiring, conflict resolution, computer systems, marketing, customer relations, customer service, employee management and event management.

After seven years with The Shangri-la Group, Laura was approached to join a hospitality consulting company based out of Atlanta, GA, 2 Places At 1 Time. She held several positions during her four years with that company, as a Client Relations Manager, Recruiting Consultant, and Implementation Specialist, gaining immeasurable practical knowledge.

Working from her home office in Vancouver, she tele-commuted with colleagues, clients and employees throughout North America. Often "on the road" three weeks out of a month, Laura wore many hats, from recruiting, hiring and training new hires, to writing training manuals and preparing marketing materials, from presentations to existing and potential clients, to nurturing existing client relationships, and implementing service to new clients, all the while managing up to 40 employees at a time. During her tenure, her client list included 3 Com Corporation, Accenture, Arthur Andersen, Ceridian, El Paso Energy, Enron, Ernst & Young, Genentech, General Electric, McKinsey & Co., PricewaterhouseCoopers, and Scotiabank.

The top values of Leading Advisor are:

- Attraction
- Currency/Energy
- Encouragement
- Partnering/People
- Professionalism/Quality/Service
- Sense/Wisdom
- Teaching
- Understanding/Empathy
- Venture

Our vision is to help our clients and their teams feel fulfilled through the development, realization and enactment of their values, vision, mission and purpose. We define fulfillment as a deep, soul-orientated feeling experienced in expressing your values, and being yourself.

Our purpose is to seek wisdom, provide encouragement, and teach understanding. And, our mission is to connect, encourage and renew the fulfillment within all people that we serve.

Part 1:

The Unmet Needs Disease

Chapter 1:

Introduction

You are an established and successful financial advisor...

Yet, are you facing roadblocks as you struggle to get to the next level? Are you bouncing against a barrier that you cannot break through?

Would you like to Clear Your Roadblocks?

As you try to navigate through the cumulative demands of clients, sales, personnel, market-driven changes in profitability, niche marketing and service requirements, you are facing these huge roadblocks:

- Lack of focus
- Not enough money coming in
- Loss of motivation
- Failure to ask for referrals
- Too many small clients and small products
- Administrative "busy work" that takes all your time

- Conflict and disputes with clients, partners, management, associates and staff
- Beating yourself up

...which all means you are working long hours and have no time to relax. You are disillusioned by business systems that are not working and by a lack of enthusiasm for your business.

The material in this book is the missing link to understanding the roadblocks that many financial advisors face in the industry. In its pages are the key ingredients to building a thriving financial advisor practice.

We have an expression here at Leading Advisor: "The client does the work, the client does the work, the client does the work."

I guarantee that if you read this book and complete the assignments, you will Clear Your Roadblocks or I will gladly refund your money.

Just one catch: to get your refund, you will have to send us written copies of the work you did on all of the assignments. I can't do this work for you.

I'd like to invite you to take just one step with me. The first step in any journey is the hardest, but with my help, you can take that step and establish the momentum that might just change your business and your life.

Are you ready for that step?

Read on.

Are you ready for "the new market"?

Whatever you want to call what we have been experiencing, whether it be slowdown, sluggish market or debacle, we are in it. What the heck, we might as well call it a recession. There, I've said it, recession, recession, recession. And now I'm over it.

I was brought up Catholic, and my parents saw to it that I went to a Catholic school. I was taught mostly by priests and nuns, and I was also an altar boy. I'm thankful for the blessing of this education and experience because it helped lay the foundational values that I have today.

Catholicism talks about the notion of limbo, a place somewhere between heaven and hell. And, while we are in this slowdown, sluggish market, debacle, that's deciding whether or not to be a recession, we are in a similar state of limbo. Everyone waits around doing nothing, watching to see what the other person will do.

Finally, the recession hits. Now, we're in hell. Past recessions have lasted 6-18 months, so the worst-case scenario is that we will be out of it soon. But, who knows?

The point is, let's get on with it.

If it's going to be, it's up to me

Did you know that the Chinese symbol for the word *crisis* is made up of two separate symbols for the words *danger* and *opportunity*?

How are you going to find the opportunity in this time of financial crisis?

How can you differentiate yourself in this new market?

Don't limit your thinking to see only the crisis and danger; that's your *Unmet Needs*, fear and negative beliefs talking.

Tap into your strength and look for the opportunities and possibilities available to today's financial advisors.

"If money is supposed to make you happy, why is nobody smiling?" Robert M. Gignac and Michael J. Townshend, *Rich is a State of Mind*

I'm sad and excited about the financial advisor profession

The dangers:

So why aren't more financial advisors jumping out of bed with excitement every day? This is the money business, after all. Why aren't they more inspired to build the foundations of a successful business? Why are they dragging their tails? Where's the light in their eyes?

We're losing advisors

- About one-third of Canada's financial advisors have already passed age 60, according to research from Advisor.ca.

- Not many young people from Generations X and Y choose to enter the industry.
- We are facing shortages similar to those doctors and accountants are already seeing.
- 23% of advisors over 63 years of age have no succession plan. Of the 67% of advisors who DO, I'm willing to bet that they're written on a restaurant napkin.
- Many advisors also have a false sense of security that selling their "book of business" (client list) is a viable succession plan. However, with fewer financial advisors coming onto the scene, advisors with 10–20 years of experience may not want to waste their time buying a book of business when they can simply attract and prospect clients who are not served because there are not enough experienced and qualified financial advisors to go around.

Some advisors are struggling

A July 2004 survey of 579 Canadian financial advisors by CEG Worldwide revealed that:

- 20% of Financial Advisors earn more than $200,000 annually

- 34% of Financial Advisors earn over $100,000 annually

Some clients are not satisfied

Advisor Impact's 2008 Economics of Loyalty Study revealed that:

- 41% of "engaged" clients give their advisor full marks, compared with...

- 30% overall, who say they are "content" with their advisors

What about the other 29% of the clients?

Without a vision and a business plan, some financial advisors are addicted to selling. They are caught in the trap of chasing sales of masses of sometimes ineffective products instead of focusing on selected profitable products. Their focus is on their own *Unmet Needs* and not on adding value to the client.

Client needs, industry regulations and investment products are becoming more and more complex. There is volatility in the market and new technology to master. Clients have access to more information and thus have higher expectations.

The opportunities:

Opportunities for succession

Retiring financial advisors with successful businesses have a lot of wisdom to pass on, but only if they look at the big picture and plan for it. It's time to stop being just a salesperson and become a business person. This means focusing on the big picture.

Malcolm Gladwell, best-selling author of *The Tipping Point,* said, "We have to recognize as a society, that 65 is an unrealistic retirement age and we have to get people to work longer." (The Globe and Mail Report on Business, October 1, 2007)

The reinvention movement

Many baby boomers have spent years in a career or job that they didn't really like; they did it to make ends meet. Now they are 50 to 60 years old and looking for something more inspiring. As one young retiree put it, "You can only go on so many cruises and have so many golf games before you get sick of it."

They have all of this experience and creativity they would like to pour into a business or career that they love, and they will be receiving substantial funds from the sale of their last business or an early buyout.

You have an extraordinary opportunity to recruit, coach, guide, mentor and teach these folks. Forget fulfillment 55, you could be contributing and inspiring others until 75 or older; how fulfilling would that be? THIS is your succession plan. Remember, "If it's going to be, it's up to me." Has the time come for a "Fulfillment Planner?"

If you already have a junior advisor in place, congratulations. Treat them well. However, if you are focusing all of your recruitment efforts on the folks from Generation X and Y, that may be a mistake. Wealthy clients simply do not want young, inexperienced advisors practicing on them. In addition, many of these Gen-X and Gen-Yers just do not have the patience to build the long term relationships and foundational business strategies necessary for success.

Opportunities for success

A 2006 British Columbia report indicated there were 55,000 business owners in B.C. between 55 and

65 years of age. Only 8% of them have a succession plan. There is a huge need for inspired and qualified advisors, and there is a huge opportunity for the cream to rise to the top.

The first baby boomer turned 60 on January 1st, 2006. As David Foot remarked when he opened the October 2007 Independent Financial Brokers Fall Summit in Toronto, only two out of ten baby boomers have a financial advisor. All you need to do is show up, and you are going to see a tsunami of opportunity coming towards you in the next fifteen years. Baby boomers are coming into billions of dollars through inheritance, the sale of businesses and early buyouts.

Nurture marketing and the wealth management movement

A July 2004 survey of 579 Canadian financial advisors by CEG Worldwide revealed that:

- 44.7% of financial advisors making over $200K are using referrals to find wealthy clients.
- 35.7% of financial advisors making between $100K and $200K are using referrals to find wealthy clients.
- 18.6% of financial advisors who are making between $50K and $100K are using referrals and they are not effectively finding wealthy clients.

These unsuccessful advisors are likely still relying heavily on push marketing's ineffective strategies. "Push marketing" is about cold calling, direct mail and newspaper advertising, and selling great quantities of potentially ineffective products to the masses.

Advisors who embrace the new wealth management movement use "nurture marketing," or "pull marketing," which includes asking for referrals on a regular basis and educating their clients that the advisor builds their business through referrals.

They find a niche where they can solve a problem, write about those solutions in a website, e-newsletter and blog and develop their writing into magazine and newspaper articles. They create seminars and speaking presentations and share their solutions with thousands of people in their niche, and never have to do another cold call again.

They create deep consultative relationships with their niche clientele of affluent clients. They deliver individualized and systematized financial planning solutions including investment management, financial planning, retirement planning, estate planning, tax planning, asset protection and cash flow and debt management. There is also a transition from commission to asset-based fee compensation structures.

In essence, it's not about selling, it's about advising.

"I have found our working relationship to be of exceptional quality and I would not be where I am today without your coaching expertise."

Tracy Valgardsson Enns, CFP, FDS, EPC
Partners In Planning
Athabasca Financial
Moose Jaw, SK

Chapter 2:
Getting Started

First, clear your roadblocks

Harry Beckwith, international speaker and best-selling author, tells us, "Storytelling is a primary means by which we convey what we do, especially in financial services where it is hard for purchasers and prospects to understand precisely what it is that you do and the value of what you do."

So, I'm going to tell you a story about a defining moment in my own life. I share it every time I do a presentation, because it will show you exactly why we start with your roadblocks.

I was eight years old. I came home from school and settled in front of the TV to watch Superman, when my mother came to me and said, "I don't want to worry you, but there's no money. There's no money for groceries, there's no money for Christmas. Your father has gone and done it again."

My father was an entrepreneur. He was a great guy; my goodness, he was loved by everyone. But, he made the mistakes that most entrepreneurs make:

- He did not take the time to plan.
- He worked very hard and often felt used by all of the clients that he was trying to serve for little or no money.
- He was better at buying things to sell than he was at selling the things that he had bought.
- He did not ask for the order.
- He did not qualify the people that he was trying to do business with.
- He worked very hard to please clients who brought in little or no money, and then he felt resentful and frustrated.
- He was constantly doing favors.
- He was trying to sell too many products.
- He did not delegate; instead, he did $5 and $10/hour work himself.
- He sacrificed family time to chase after potential business. I remember waiting and waiting for him to pick us up after church or cub scouts.

I was an only child and my mother needed to talk. So, I'm the one she came to with her worries about money. From that point on, I believed there was no money. In my mind, I had to become the breadwinner of the family.

I started with a paper route. By the time I was twelve, I had the three biggest morning dailies in the city. I was working it. The old timers would come up to me and say, "You have got what it takes. You are going to make it." I kept on going; paper routes, mowing lawns and shoveling snow. In the process, I gave up my childhood, friendships, education and having fun.

A buddy and I even spent our Saturdays unloading 24 ton trailers of alfalfa bales from Ellensburg, Washington (I grew up in the Fraser Valley of British Columbia, Canada). Those things weighed 140 pounds each. Yup, I was driven.

Continuing to believe there was no money, I carried this same fear into my adult working life. It drove me to become what I call today an obsessive *super sales person* with everything I touched. Give me a sales record and I could break it.

In the process, I gave up my first marriage, my friendships and my family. By 1994, I was bankrupt, both financially and emotionally. I lost my business. That was when I learned that the sales and marketing I'd worked so hard to master were not the most important business activities after all.

I learned that the work I had to do was to clear my *Unmet Needs*, negative emotions and negative beliefs. I had to rewrite the story that was based on fear, the story that there was no money. Otherwise, I would just keep playing out the same thing again and again.

I had to clear those roadblocks in order to lay the foundation of a successful business and a meaningful life. And, so do you.

I dedicated the rest of my professional life to helping others avoid the same mistakes that I made. Today, I have a successful coaching practice and my goals for 2010 include:

- Revenues in the mid-6 figures
- 12 weeks of vacation
- Three-day weekends in the weeks that I work
- Doing only what I love - speaking, coaching and writing
- Enjoying a support team of seven people who are responsible for the key performance activities of the business - finance, information technology, marketing and sales, resource development, website development and most importantly of all...
- Clients like you who rave about the difference we've made in their lives.

Maybe you don't need to Clear Your Roadblocks. Maybe you are satisfied with your business. Maybe you are JPL. Ok, I'm being smart here, JPL stands for just plain lazy. The point is, I'm here to help the people who understand that there is far more available than they are currently getting. They are ready to implement a proven, sustainable system for business success.

Maybe you can identify some of the roadblocks that have held you back, maybe not. The point is, you know you have been bumping into the same old issues time and time again, and you are ready to do something different.

Albert Einstein said, "We can't solve problems by using the same kind of thinking we used when we created them," and that the definition of insanity is doing the same thing over and over again but expecting different results.

I am here for those of you are who are honest and are saying, "I am stuck and I need to do something about it." You are ready to get out of the *comfort zone.*

Why motivation doesn't work

You have heard other coaches, authors and experts talk about the foundational pieces you need in order to have a successful and profitable business. You know you need a business plan. You know you need a vision.

You have bought their books and attended their seminars. You may have your very own shrine of these materials in your office. There are some great ones on my own shelves: *Rich Dad, Poor Dad, Think and Grow Rich, The Purpose-Driven Life, The Seven Habits of Highly Effective People.* Sometimes, even just looking at them up there gives you a little jolt of motivation. But, does it last, or are you still stuck?

I have seen the motivational business from both sides of the stage. As the owner of a highly regarded, successful personal and professional development company, I was a popular speaker. I attended just about every personal and professional development course known to man. Everyone, myself included, regarded me as an expert on time management, finance, sales, marketing, leadership and personal development.

Then, in 1994, I lost the business. It was a major shock; not only to me, but also to everyone who knew me.

You see, motivation can work, but it doesn't last - it is unsustainable. That's why I've dedicated my life since then to creating a sustainable system for a successful and profitable business.

Motivation fails because it is inherently flawed. It is based on fear; fear of losing something you already have, or fear of not getting something that you want.

I looked up motive in the dictionary, and it said motive comes from a place of need, desire or fear. So, you see, the whole premise of motivation is flawed. You have to hit bottom before you can turn around and become motivated.

Look at the word desire, as well. It comes from the Latin word *desidus*, which means moving away from the star. You are already a star. These things are sabotaging you.

No matter how motivated you are, you cannot progress past a certain point until you address your *Unmet Need Disease.*

If you are looking for motivation from this book, look elsewhere. I'm not trying to motivate you; I'm trying to cure you. What I offer is a proven, sustainable model of success that will address your *Unmet Needs Disease,* spark your aspirations and give you the inspiration – not motivation – to put it to use.

Maslow's hierarchy of needs

5. Growth Needs – Self Actualization
4. Esteem Needs – Self Esteem, Recognition, Status
3. Social Needs – Sense of Belonging, Love - Approval
2. Safety Needs – Security, Protection – Safety
1. Physiological Needs – Hunger, Thirst

Abraham Maslow was an American psychologist who studied healthy, successful, extraordinary people - he called them self-actualized. He looked for what they had in common and developed a theory of human behavior. The result was the hierarchy of needs, which you see above.

It was during my training at Coach U (1995-1998) that I developed and honed some of my concepts about *Unmet Needs*. My previous experience with motivational training taught me that if you had a negative belief, all you had to do was change it to a positive belief. However, this proved to be unsustainable, which was very unsettling for me.

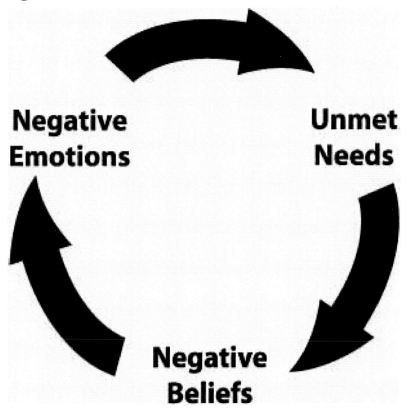

Through this work, I discovered the missing link. It was the connection between the *Unmet Need* and the emotions and negative beliefs. You need to identify the *Unmet Need* that the emotions and negative beliefs relate to. Clear that *Unmet Need,* negative emotion and negative beliefs all at the same time.

Maslow's concept is that until you meet the lower needs, you cannot express your values. Your *Unmet Needs* will dominate and run you until they are identified and satisfied. No matter how close you get to success and to the next level of growth, you'll bump up against those *Unmet Needs* and they'll catapult you back to where you started.

Unmet Needs create negative emotions. It is virtually impossible to feel confident and positive about an area where you have an *Unmet Need.* These *Unmet Needs* and negative emotions subconsciously and unconsciously run at the core of many financial advisors, who often become stuck at levels two or three.

Level two is our safety needs. If you have an *Unmet Need* for safety, you will have negative emotions about safety and security. You are going to be anxious. You are going to be thinking, "I don't have enough time," or "I don't have enough money." What kind of an advisor will that make you? Are you going to be 100% present with your clients? No, you are going to be distracted.

If you have an *Unmet Need* for safety, writes Maslow, you will have "a fear of knowing," since your negative thinking would have you believe the worst is going to happen. As a form of self-medicating, you keep busy, so you do not have to face the negative reality you have invented in your subconscious mind.

A good example of this is delegating. I constantly hear advisors moaning and complaining about all of the paperwork on their desk. What is one of the number one things that the Million Dollar Round Table (MDRT) tells you to do? Delegate. Stop doing $5, $10, $15, $20 and $25/hour work. Of course, in order to delegate you need someone to delegate to. Why don't you invest in that support for your business? Why do we get caught up in busy work and complain about it? Because we're driven by our *Unmet Need* for safety.

Level three is our social needs, our sense of belonging and love. This need cannot and should not be met by your clients; it must come from you. There is all this talk about getting high net worth clients, yet advisors don't approach them or try to solicit their business. What are your negative emotions about that? You feel anxious and fearful. What are your negative beliefs about that? That you are not good enough, that you do not know enough, that you do not have enough education. Therefore, you do nothing.

You'll see how *Unmet Needs* are impacting **your** success by completing The Clear Values Scorecard in the next chapter.

"Another business coach may have worked with me through the business plan only to have the issues continue to interfere with the plan. Simon's Clear Your Roadblocks Program allowed me to hit the nail right on the head."

Donald Daggett
Associate Investment Advisor
CIBC Wood Gundy
Windsor, ON

Chapter 3:

Are you a Financial Survivor or a Financial Advisor?

Evolution has programmed us to feel the fear for survival in our guts. In days gone by, our survival was dependent upon our tribe. The tribe reinforced obedience and conformity to the tribal system through the threat of expulsion. Expulsion from the tribe meant certain death.

The tribal mind is primal, hooked into that basest of instincts – survival itself. It focuses on the negative and messages such as, "things are scarce" and, "there isn't enough to go around." The primal mind is always poised to fight and expects constant attacks.

The captive agency system, which introduced many financial advisors to the profession, is a tribal system. Remaining a member of today's financial advisor tribe can mean meeting specific sales targets. The negative ego mind perceives that not meeting these sales targets means expulsion from the tribe and is a definite risk to survival.

Many of the captive agencies no longer exist. More and more financial advisors have decided either to become independent, or have been forced to become independent. However, even independent advisors can be triggered into thinking with this survival-based negative ego mind.

Financial Survivors suffer from the *Unmet Needs Disease*, causing the negative emotion and the negative belief that they are not achieving their true potential as an advisor.

Financial Advisors have Clear Values, causing the positive feeling and the positive belief they are achieving their true potential as an advisor.

Note: Some of the above ideas were developed from Steven Pressfield's book, The War of Art. Steven also wrote the novel, The Legend of Bagger Vance, which was adapted into a must-see movie starring Matt Damon and Will Smith.

The missing link

Industry experts agree that the key foundational pieces for a successful business are:

- Values
- Vision, Purpose, Mission
- Money Management Plan
- Time Management Plan
- 90-day Goals
- Action Steps
- Project Management System

Most people, financial advisors included, don't understand the importance of their values. Values are the DNA of the vision and the vision is the DNA of the business plan, all of which helps the financial advisor become a Leading Advisor in the industry. Without values, the entire plan will be misguided. An even greater challenge occurs when *Unmet Needs* dominate your values and create negative emotions and beliefs.

The problem with most personal and professional development programs is they present these steps in the wrong order. Worse, they don't address *Unmet Needs* at all. That is the missing link.

The Clear Values Scorecard

To fully understand your current situation, complete *The Clear Values Scorecard*. Rate your position between each pair of phrases. Decide where you lie on the scale from 1 to 10. Add up your total from each column.

	Financial Survivor											Financial Advisor
1	I lack focus.	1	2	3	4	5	6	7	8	9	10	I follow a written 5-year vision and business plan.
2	I am not making as much money as I would like.	1	2	3	4	5	6	7	8	9	10	I am fully satisfied with the amount of money I am making.
3	I have to get myself pumped when I am selling.	1	2	3	4	5	6	7	8	9	10	I feel naturally excited about my work and I enjoy the selling process.

		1	2	3	4	5	6	7	8	9	10	
4	I feel I am not getting enough referrals.	1	2	3	4	5	6	7	8	9	10	I am getting many great, qualified referrals.
5	I feel that I am working too hard, with too many unqualified or C and D clients.	1	2	3	4	5	6	7	8	9	10	I am getting many new high-quality clients.
6	I try to serve anyone and everyone.	1	2	3	4	5	6	7	8	9	10	I have branded my business and I am focused on a niche market.
7	I do too many favors and I sell too many products.	1	2	3			6	7	8	9		I am focused on profitable products and services.
8	I feel completely overwhelmed, doing things I don't like to do.	1	2	3	4	5	6	7	8	9	10	I do what I love to do and have a hiring system to delegate everything else.
9	I have a lot of conflict in my business relationships.	1	2	3	4	5	6	7	8	9	10	I manage my business relationships extremely well.
10	I beat myself up when things don't go right and I have lost my enthusiasm for my business.	1	2	3	4	5	6	7	8	9	10	I always celebrate my successes and learn from my setbacks. I am achieving my true potential as an advisor.
	ADD COLUMN TOTALS											YOUR SCORE _____

Were most of your answers closer to the left-hand (survivor) or the right-hand (advisor) side of the scorecard?

Why do you think that is?

Is what you have been doing to improve your business working?

What do you think would move your score closer to the right-hand side?

Let's look at Item 4. Where did you score along the continuum between, "I feel I am not getting enough referrals," to, "I am getting many great qualified referrals"? If you are farther to the left than you want to be, I have one question for you: **are you asking for referrals**?

Experts say the number one marketing strategy to build your business is asking for referrals. It is one of the most efficient and economical ways to build a service-based business. Yet, when I survey an audience of advisors, they tell me they're only asking for referrals about a third of the time, if that much.

Here is a step-by-step explanation of how your *Unmet Needs* affect your score on this question:

1. Asking for referrals triggers your *Unmet Need* for approval.
2. Your *Unmet Need* for approval generates the negative emotions of anxiety or fear.
3. These negative emotions generate the negative beliefs, "I'm not good enough," "I don't know enough," or "The client might say no."

4. The anxiety and fear continue to trigger the *Unmet Need* for safety and approval and lock in the negative beliefs.
5. You don't ask for the referral, OR (worse) your client picks up on the *Unmet Need*, negative emotions and negative beliefs and that affects his or her confidence in you as an advisor.

In his book, *Mind Power*, John Kehoe teaches that thoughts are real forces, and that, "Whatever you believe, you are right." Your negative beliefs emanate from you like radio waves, and your clients receive them. They don't refer you because they've picked up that lack of belief in yourself. Why would they trust and believe in you if you don't?

Imagine, just for a moment, what asking for referrals might be like if you were NOT inhibited by your *Unmet Needs*:

1. You would be in touch with your values of abundance, attraction, energy and service.
2. You would feel the positive emotions of excitement, energy, joy and passion.
3. You would focus on the positive belief that, "My clients receive great value from the products and services that I offer."
4. You would ask for and receive many referrals. All clients want to do business with advisors who have energy and passion. Moreover, they'll feel good about referring you to others because you'll make *them* look good for discovering you.

"Your values based approach has provided me with a number of tangible benefits and has given me a solid foundation to accelerate the growth and success of DBS. Your services exceeded my expectations."

Paul Ghezzi, CA
Founder
DBS Private Client Group Inc.
Markham, ON

Chapter 4:

What You Need to Do

Wake up and smell the ego

You already know what to do, so why aren't you doing it? Why are you so stuck?

I say it is because you are asleep. You have fallen asleep and let your primal, negative ego mind take over your consciousness. In days gone by, your primal negative ego mind had two thoughts: "What am I going to eat?" and "What wild beast is going to eat me?"

One client likened the negative ego mind to the appendix. They believed the appendix was a vestigial organ left over from a time when our ancestors had to digest leaves and raw meat. So, on the plus side, the negative ego is an organ that stopped us from becoming raw meat. It is a left over safety mechanism that protects us when there's a threat of being hurt.

Today, the financial advisor's negative ego mind is thinking, "How am I going to make my payments?"

or "I should have listened to my mother and stayed in a regular job with benefits." Zig Ziegler and Stuart Smalley (the Al Franken character from Saturday Night Live) both called this "stinkin' thinkin'."

In his book *The Power of Intention* (2004), Dr. Wayne Dyer tells us that the ego is made up of the following ingredients:

1. I am what I have. My possessions define me.
2. I am what I do. My achievements define me.
3. I am what others think of me. My reputation defines me.
4. I am separate from everyone. My body defines me alone.
5. I am separate from all that is missing in my life. My life space is disconnected from my desires.
6. I am separate from God. My life depends on God's assessment of my worthiness.

With its obsession of outside perceptions for what others think of possessions, achievements, reputation, body image, life image and worthiness, the all consuming negative ego blocks communication .

You were born perfect, perfectly awake and capable of seeing the beautiful, positive side of the world. Most of the time, your physiological, educational, emotional and spiritual needs were met by your parents.

Then one day, you turned to them and were met by, "What are you bothering me for?" All of a sudden, you were dealing with pain and separation. Your negative ego mind was born to cope with your *Unmet Need* for worthiness.

When you think about asking for a referral, there's a risk involved. Therefore, your internal safety mechanism - your negative ego mind - comes alive and chimes in with the negative emotions of fear and the negative beliefs that will stop you from taking the risk. "I can't ask for a referral," it says, "I'm not good enough, I don't know enough, and the guy might reject me."

So what do you do? Nothing. You stay asleep.

When you were belittled or passed over by your parents, you didn't get that need met, and that led to emotions of shame. Fast forward to today, and that manifests in negative thoughts of how you are not good enough, leading to the actions of chasing money and possessions, leading to more emptiness, failure and *Unmet Needs*. In your pursuit of what is missing, you miss more.

You need to wake up and take back control of your emotions and thinking. Give your negative ego mind a rest and set your sights on a higher level of feeling and thinking.

When you address your *Unmet Needs*, you master your emotions and wrestle control from your negative ego mind. You can win at any game you play. Picture Tiger Woods winning the U.S. Open. Consider that for the rest of us, there are three choices when it comes to playing the game of life:

1. Staying on the sidelines and opting not to play at all.
2. Struggling to play the game while being hampered by negative emotions and beliefs generated by *Unmet Needs*.
3. Playing to win and then triumphantly

experiencing and sharing your feelings when they do (as Tiger Woods did).

Please keep in mind that an *Unmet Need* can be both a blessing and a curse. Being a young boy trying to sort out the trials and tribulations of my family drama left me with an *Unmet Need* for approval. That has turned out to be a catalyst for the valuable work that my clients receive from me today.

They appreciate my ability and drive to help them sort out complex situations in a short time, complete with an action plan. My *Unmet Need* for approval was like a grain of sand in the oyster; after many years of irritation, a beautiful pearl emerged. That is what I am blessed with today.

Suspend judgment

Stephen Covey invites us to, "seek first to understand."

What does he mean by that?

Instead of trying to fit everything and everyone into your set version of how life works, open your mind to new possibilities and understand that everybody else has their own version of how life works.

Otherwise, you waste precious time and energy in judgment of the people and things that you don't understand, and you miss out on opportunities to learn, grow and prosper.

Start now, with this book. When you read something that challenges what you always thought or what you have always done, you have two choices:

1. You can judge the hell out of me for suggesting something so crazy, or
2. You can learn and try something new and get better results than you have been getting.

Do you know who said, "When you believe you can do it, you can do it?" Notice how the quote emphasizes, "you, you, you?" Can you guess? Was it Mahatma Gandhi? Wayne Dwyer? Deepak Chopra? Dr. Robert Schuler?

Actually, it was none of the above. It wasn't a spiritual guru at all. It was a hockey guru, by the name of Wayne Gretzky (and it was in a television commercial). A regular, ordinary guy. You don't have to be a spiritual person to understand and use this material. So open your mind and join me.

When there is no understanding, there is judgment. When there is judgment, there can be no understanding. Judgment and no understanding are what cause you to create the roadblocks to your success.

Get uncomfortable

In a wonderful book called, *The Alchemist* by Paulo Coelho, the shepherd asked the alchemist if there was anything he still needed to know.

"What you still need to know is this: before a dream is realized, the Soul of the World tests everything that was learned along the way. It does this not because it is evil, but so we can, in addition to realizing our dreams, master the lessons we've learned as we've moved toward that dream. That's the point at which most people give up. It's the point at which, as we say in the language of the desert, one 'dies of thirst just when the palm trees have appeared on the horizon.'"

We're tested by the world as we get closer and closer to our dreams. Things can get pretty sticky; it is called the Discomfort Zone. However, you can't get around it, you have to go through it. "No pain, no gain," as they say.

According to Chris Barrow, a world-class business coach who works exclusively with dentists in the UK:

"If you want to achieve a resolution that has integrity and sustainability, you simply must enter the Discomfort Zone. Any resolution that has sidestepped this area will collapse at some point.

Crossing the Discomfort Zone requires courage, commitment and bigger thinking than you have ever needed before. However, you don't have to do it alone; this is where a trained coach comes in to lead you into the Breakthrough Zone.

The Breakthrough Zone is a high-energy place that feels liberating, light, unburdened, open and creative. This is the land of a-ha moments and light bulbs going off over your head."

The cover story of Fast Company Magazine's May 2005 issue, "Change or Die," caught my attention. While Alan Deutschman writes about the topic primarily from a medical perspective, he offers the disheartening fact that whether you are trying to make changes in your personal or business lives, your chance of failure is over 90%.

For example, 90% of people two years after coronary artery bypass grafting have not changed their lifestyle, including the top five unhealthiest indulgences of too much smoking, drinking, eating, stress and sitting around. Doctors have told these patients that they're putting themselves at risk, but *even the fear of death did not motivate them to change.*

The fact is, we resist change not just because it is uncomfortable; we resist change because our current behaviors, thoughts and habits are helping us cope, however badly, with life. They are helping us cope with our negative emotions, such as fear - fear of death, fear of failure and fear of financial ruin.

Plan and envision

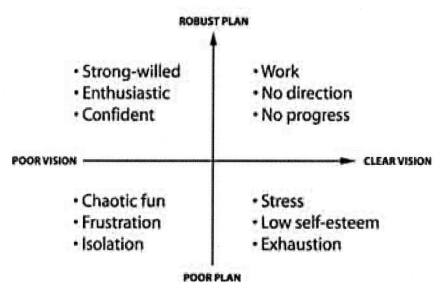

The above matrix is ©copyright by Chris Barrow, and used with permission.

"Have a vision not clouded by fear."
Cherokee Proverb

As you can see on this chart, it is very, very important to have both a strong plan and a strong vision, and for them to be integrated and working together.

The late great Thomas Leonard, founder of Coach University, gave us these definitions:

Vision is about what you see as possible.

Purpose is how you are going to be, to further that possibility.

Mission (plan) is what you are going to do, to make that vision happen.

"Fear not that your life will someday end.
Fear only that you do nothing with it."
Unknown

Think bigger

Why haven't you had a plan or a vision up until now? Because the minute you think about your vision, you immediately think about the world around you.

It used to be, that would bring up images of peace on earth, cars with tail fins with lots of power, the house with the white picket fence, Sunday, Monday, Happy Days with Fonzie and Richie and Joanie Cunningham.

Ed Sullivan was introducing, "Ladies and gentlemen, The Beatles," and Paul McCartney was singing, "Yesterday."

But today, what are you thinking about? All of the world's problems:

- Climate change
- Crime
- Disease
- Economy
- Electrical shortages
- Exploding shampoo bottles
- Homelessness
- Hunger
- Oil shortages
- Terrorism
- War

We turn on the television set and watch the news and get bombarded some more with stories about all of those things. Why do we turn on the news? Why are we addicted to these stories? Why does misery love company?

Because, when we think about other people's problems, it distracts us from thinking about our own. It helps us to cope by saying, "My problems are not that bad, look at how bad their problems are."

We can go back to our sleepwalk through life, doing the same thing over and over again while expecting a different result. We stick our heads in the sand, we cope and we just do the stuff that's easy. We're being financial survivors, not financial advisors.

Your vision is the solution.

Think about your clients. You can create an extraordinary difference for your clients when you can think bigger, strengthen yourself from the inside out and get your vision in order. Remember that saying; "If it's going to be, it's up to me?"

When David walked onto the battlefield to face Goliath, most people said, "My goodness look, he's going to get killed for sure!" It was the people with vision who said, "Look how big that sucker is, David can't miss!" And, one shot was all it took. David had vision. Right? It was Goliath's forehead. One shot. That's what it took. He was committed.

Show your clients that you have vision, that you are thinking bigger, that you are thinking beyond the bad news - both for their sake and for your own sake. When you are "walking your talk," people will be drawn to you.

Vision is about what you see as possible for others in the world. Vision is about what you can do to help make that happen. Vision is about serving the needs of others, not fulfilling your own. The magical thing is, when you do define that vision, it will have an extraordinary impact on your own life as well. Your vision will pull you forward and make all your dreams come true.

> *"Do not let your fire go out, spark by irreplaceable spark... Do not let the hero in your soul perish, in lonely frustration for the life you deserved, but have never been able to reach. Check your road and the nature of your battle. The world you desired can be won. It exists, it is real, it is possible, it is yours."*
> Ayn Rand

"I would like to thank you for the help you have already provided. That one realization is worth the price of the whole program. I look forward to the next steps."

Grant McPhail
Rice Financial Group
Brandon, MB

Chapter 5:

The Biggest Roadblocks of All - Your Unmet Needs

What is the Unmet Needs Disease?

The *Unmet Needs Disease* is an overgrowth of negative emotions and beliefs. It leads to ineffective behavior and an inability to conceive or carry out a strong vision and plan. This, in turn, inhibits the fulfillment of dreams and stunts financial, emotional and personal growth.

You see, as we've discussed already, successful people get positive results by having a strong vision and a strong plan. They fulfill that vision and plan by carrying out positive behaviors. Those positive behaviors stem from positive feelings and beliefs, and those positive feelings and beliefs stem from knowing and expressing their values.

Coming from another angle, you might say the key to success is knowing and expressing your values, which leads to positive feelings and beliefs, which leads to positive behaviors, which leads to the fulfillment of your vision and plan.

Most financial advisors do not know what their values are. They can't see that their behavior is actually driven by their *Unmet Needs*, and therefore is in conflict with their positive values (that are under the surface). That's why they're not getting the results they say they want.

Is it a value or an Unmet Need?

We are all hardwired to try to satisfy our *Unmet Needs* for safety, approval, recognition and respect from outside of ourselves. However, it can't be done. It's impossible. You must stop and learn how to meet the needs yourself. The negative emotions go away. The negative beliefs go away. Your values start to show up and be expressed in your life. While values run deep within us, *Unmet Needs* easily overshadow them. Values are like an ostrich. What do I mean by that? Well, they only lift their head out of the sand when it's safe. If your *Unmet Needs* are screaming for attention, your values will stay hidden.

As a values and behavioral analyst, when I start working with new clients, I produce a 37-page report identifying their values and their behaviors. Time and again, I see how surprised people are because they had no idea what their values were and they weren't conscious of their behaviors.

I help them to see that their values and behaviors are actually in conflict. It's like having one foot on the gas and one foot on the brake. It's just not going to work. You can't propel yourself forward, and what's more, your entire guidance system is off.

Remember, your values will stay unexpressed and even unknown, as long as there are *Unmet Needs* in the picture. That's why motivation and personal development fails. You cannot slap an "I'm happy," affirmation on top of an *Unmet Need* and expect to live out that value of happiness.

You also can't get rid of *Unmet Needs* by drinking, drugging, eating, partying, shopping or gambling them away. These are all different versions of the same misguided attempt to get what you really need (safety, approval, recognition and belonging). It won't work and you will only attract more conflict, rejection, struggle, suffering and time-consuming tasks and people.

Most advisors, and people in general, do not know the difference between a value and an *Unmet Need*. Politicians, for example, may stand on a podium and tell us about their "family values," and then a few months later we're watching them give a press conference trying to explain a sex scandal. The thing is, they might have truly believed in those values at some level, but their family values were in hiding while they chased after their *Unmet Needs*. It happens to many of us (just not necessarily on television).

Look at money, for example. When negative emotions surrounding money are an expression of your *Unmet Need* for safety, as in anxiety and fear combined with negative beliefs of "I will never have enough money," you will continually attract uncertain situations and people. You'll feel anxious, edgy, fearful, hesitant, jittery, nervous, panicky, reluctant, restless, scared, shaky, skeptical, suspicious and uneasy about money.

When positive feelings about money are an expression of your value of abundance, the process of attracting money flows effortlessly and you feel confident and hopeful about your prospects. You focus on the positive beliefs that, "There is an abundance of business," and, "There is an abundance of currency." You continually succeed and accomplish great things, while attracting successful situations and people. You feel alive, amazed, animated, appreciative, blissful, cheerful, comfortable, confident, delighted, ecstatic, encouraged, energetic, enthusiastic, excited, exhilarated, fascinated, gleeful, glorious, happy, inspired, joyful, loving, optimistic, peaceful, radiant, satisfied, stimulated and wonderful. When was the last time you experienced these feelings?

Unmet Needs and the Law of Attraction

One day, an old, Native American grandfather was talking to his grandson. He said, "There are two wolves fighting inside all of us - the wolf of fear and hate, and the wolf of love and peace."

The grandson listened, then looked up at his grandfather and asked, "Which one will win?"

The grandfather replied, "The one we feed."

The Universal Law of Attraction states that we attract whatever we consciously or unconsciously give our attention to - whether we want it or not.

Swiss psychologist Carl Jung gave serious study to the idea of meaningful coincidences and concluded that there are no coincidences. He called this phenomena synchronicity and believed that it is as natural a principal as cause and effect.

You potentially have two powerful phenomena working against you. First, your *Unmet Needs* are fueling your negative emotions and negative beliefs. Second, the Law of Attraction kicks in as you attract further challenges with money, conflict, rejection, struggle, suffering and time consuming tasks and people.

When you deal with your *Unmet Needs*, and identify and express your values, the accompanying positive feelings and positive beliefs will attract positive experiences and events.

The movie, *The Secret*, popularized the idea of the Law of Attraction and introduced it to a broader audience. There's an old saying, "You don't have a secret, a secret has you."

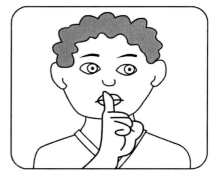

In this case, you don't have an *Unmet Need*, it has you. It is time to wake up.

Earlier, I quoted John Kehoe, author of *Mind Power*, who tells us "thoughts are real forces."

Are you saying, "I don't have enough time," "There is too much to do," or, "I'll never get it all done?" Whatever you believe, you are right, because that is what you will attract.

What if you were to adopt the belief, "I have an abundance of time for anything that I am committed to doing," instead?

The fact that we are electromagnetic beings isn't really a secret. Every first year physics student knows this. What is now coming under very careful study however is the realization that what we are feeling at any moment causes the emanation of vibrational waves.

These waves match up to corresponding tones on a piano keyboard. For example, if the vibrations generated by your current emotional and thinking state are below "middle C" on the piano, they are associated with negative emotions and beliefs, and the lower they go, the slower the vibration and the more negative they are.

If your vibrational waves correspond to middle C or higher on the piano keyboard, they're higher and faster vibrations associated with pleasure. The higher they get, the more excited they get.

That piano is us. Take even a tiny bit of fret or worry, and you are down below middle C. Take unbridled hate, and now you have dropped down into the arena of very powerful, long, slow vibrations.

Another way to demonstrate the physical effects of expressing our values (positive feelings and beliefs) versus our *Unmet Needs* (negative emotions and beliefs) comes from the scientific study of the emotional response of water.

Masaru Emoto, author of The Message from Water (http://www.hado.net/), and his team, experiment with water samples exposed to music, spoken words, words typed and taped to glass containers, photographs and long distance thought messages. Their amazing photographs of the crystallized water samples show just how greatly water is affected by positive and negative stimuli. That includes, of course, the water inside of us - anywhere from 50 to 75% of an adult's total body weight.

An advisor invoking the positive side of the Law of Attraction will:

- Offer his or her expertise (versus prospecting or trying to sell)
- Take a genuine interest (versus trying to build rapport)
- Set a selling target of twice the quota amount (versus trying to meet quota)
- Seek to serve (rather than persuade or cajole)
- Seek to educate (versus trying to sell)
- Come across as graceful and professional (versus being pushy)
- Expand the potential customer's vision, expectations and goals (versus touting features and benefits)
- Be motivated by the improvements to their clients' lives (versus their sales numbers)

- Gain most new business via referrals (versus advertisement and promotion)
- Generate new interest continually (versus marketing and prospecting in cycles)

Please note that some of the concepts above were developed from the book, *Excuse Me, Your Life Is Waiting* by Lyn Grabhorn and from the concept of "Irresistible Attraction," by the late Thomas Leonard, founder of Coach U.

The countless advisors that I've talked to all pretty much agree on what they want to attract:

- I follow a written 5-year vision and business plan, and I always have enough time.
- I am fully satisfied with the amount of money I am making.
- I feel naturally excited about my work and I enjoy the selling process.
- I am getting many great qualified referrals
- I am getting many new high quality clients.
- I have branded my business and I am focused on a niche market.
- I am focused on profitable products and services.
- I do what I love to do and have a hiring system to delegate everything else.
- I manage my business relationships extremely well.
- I always celebrate my successes, learn from my setbacks and I am achieving my true potential as an advisor.

So why is it that they're getting:

- Lack of focus
- Not enough money coming in

- Loss of motivation
- Failure to ask for referrals
- Too many small clients and small products
- Administrative "busy work" that takes all their time
- Conflict and disputes with clients, partners, management, associates and staff
- Beating themselves up

Once you understand the link between *Unmet Needs* and the Law of Attraction, it is pretty simple to see why.

"From the moment Simon was introduced to our conference, I simply knew that he was the one who would coach me to awaken the energy within myself to advance my practice and my life to where I have always felt it should be. The exercises Simon provides work if you apply yourself and work toward change."

Philip Hauser, CFPP
Sterling Mutual Funds Inc.
London, Ontario

Chapter 6:

Do You Have These Common Symptoms of the Unmet Needs Disease?

You are emotionally retired

Have you emotionally retired from your business, your personal life or both?

You know the look; you have seen it in others. There's a flatness of expression, a hesitation in words and a slouching of posture. There's no longer a light in the eyes (if there ever was), and it seems like they've given up on life. Is it happening in you?

Can you, your business, your clients or family afford for you to be emotionally retired? What do you think it's like for your clients to work with you? How much fun do you think you are around the kitchen table at the end of the day?

If emotional retirement hasn't hit you yet, is it just around the corner at 40, 45, 50, 55, 60 or 65?

The long-term solution for emotional retirement is to address your *Unmet Needs Disease*.

A short-term solution... purchase a journal and write down all of your successes, no matter how small. Think back on the day, on the week, on the month, on the quarter and on the year. Re-live each success and how they made you feel. Re-light that spark in your eyes by reconnecting with what has gone well.

You are just coping

Our unhealthy and unproductive habits aren't just more comfortable than the idea of trying something new, but as we learned from the "Change or Die" article (see Get Uncomfortable), they are coping mechanisms.

Look through this list of common coping mechanisms to see if you can spot any of your favorites:

- Acting out: not coping - giving in to the pressure to misbehave.
- Aim inhibition: lowering sights to what seems more achievable.
- Attack: trying to beat down that which is threatening you.
- Avoidance: mentally or physically avoiding something that causes distress.
- Compartmentalization: separating conflicting thoughts into separated compartments.
- Compensation: making up for a weakness in one area by gaining strength in another.
- Conversion: subconscious conversion of stress into physical symptoms.

- Denial: refusing to acknowledge that an event has occurred.
- Displacement: shifting of intended action to a safer target.
- Dissociation: separating oneself from parts of your life.
- Fantasy: escaping reality into a world of possibility.
- Idealization: playing up the good points and ignoring limitations of things desired.
- Identification: copying others to take on their characteristics.
- Intellectualization: avoiding emotion by focusing on facts and logic.
- Passive aggression: avoiding refusal by passive avoidance.
- Projection: seeing your own unwanted feelings in other people.
- Rationalization: creating logical reasons for bad behavior.
- Reaction Formation: avoiding something by taking a polar opposite position.
- Regression: returning to a child like state to avoid problems.
- Repression: subconsciously hiding uncomfortable thoughts.
- Somatization: psychological problems turned into physical symptoms.
- Sublimation: channeling psychic energy into acceptable activities.
- Suppression: consciously holding back unwanted urges.
- Symbolization: turning unwanted thoughts into metaphoric symbols.

- Trivializing: making small what is really something big.
- Undoing: actions that psychologically 'undo' wrongdoings for the wrongdoer.

The above list of coping mechanisms is (c) Davis Straker, *http://changingminds.org/explanations/behaviors/coping/coping.htm*, and used with permission.

Choosing a boat instead of an assistant

Advisors and potential coaching clients give me a lot of excuses for putting off their coaching programs. They want to end their struggle, but just not yet.

I hear similar excuses for not making other changes that would help, such as hiring an assistant. One advisor told me that he would hire an assistant, but he needs the cash to pay for a new boat.

True, the boat would do a lot to "medicate" the pain the advisor is experiencing to console him about his lack of clients and his failure to satisfy the ones he has. On the other hand, he could hire the assistant, who will take better care of his clients while freeing up his own time to attract and retain new clients, and provide the best service he can deliver.

It's all about choice. Would you rather start now to end your business struggles and begin a life of prosperity and abundance (filled with boats, if that is what you want) or get your boat now and stay stuck? The trouble with the latter choice is, you may end up living on that boat.

You are thinking like an employee

In his presentation, "The 8 Best Practices Of High-Performing Advisors" at the May 2007 Advocis Durham Education Day (Ontario), Norm Trainor remarked that there has been a big shift in the industry; from advisors being sales-driven in the 70's and 80's, to being marketing-driven in the 90's and to being customer service-driven in the new millennium.

The old sales paradigm will not work anymore, he said, as today's savvy customers are more concerned with what happens after the sale than what happens before the sale. Customers are tired of the old self-centered sales approach.

With a client-centered approach, you are more concerned about your customer than a sales bonus or commission. The bonus comes when you please your customers and they return time after time for your guidance, products and services. Therefore, advisors need to become more focused on adding value to the service they are providing to the customer.

If service, not sales, is your underlying motive, you will naturally be driven to grow, learn and improve, by investing in your ongoing professional and personal development. That leads us to our next symptom.

You don't invest in your education

Norm Trainor remarked on another big shift in the industry. In the 70's and 80's, many agencies had captive advisors, but things are very different today. Now, out of 2,000 financial institutions in Canada and the USA, only 33 agencies have captive financial advisors.

Financial advisors unknowingly adopted an employee attitude, which leaves them short sighted when it comes to making an investment in their own training. They are unconsciously waiting for "the company" to do or provide the training. They must understand that today they are the company.

In my experience, the average financial advisor will invest between $2,500 and $3,500 per year on continuing education or development. That's a far cry from the cost of something like coaching. Industry research suggests that coaching fees run from $5,000 to $25,000 per year.

Once their initial training is complete, the majority think that is it – for life. This is very sad, as there is so much value financial advisors can give back to humankind.

When I talk about education, I'm talking about three different things:

1. Professional development
2. Personal development
3. Product development

1. Professional Development

According to www.wikipedia.com, "Professional development often refers to verbal and tactile skills required for maintaining a specific career path or to general skills offered through continuing education, including the more general skills area of personal development. It can be seen as training to keep current with changing technology and practices in a profession or in the concept of lifelong learning. Developing and implementing a program of professional development is often a function of the human resources or organization development department of a large corporation or institution." (Retrieved July 7, 2008)

The last sentence of this definition identifies the symptom. It is no wonder that most financial advisors only participate in continuing education if it is given to them for free; they're not part of a large corporation or institution (as we covered in the previous symptom, "You are thinking like an employee").

When their initial training ended, some advisors adopted the positive belief that, "if it's going to be, it's up to me." They went out and continued to invest in their own professional, personal or product development and they grew and became successful.

Other advisors fell victim to their own negative beliefs, such as, "I gave this company everything and now they will not give me the time of day. Woe is me. I guess I won't be able to get any more training." Consequently, their outcome was limited growth and mediocre success.

2. Personal Development (Self Help)

It's no accident that if you search Wikipedia for "Personal Development," it leads to a definition for "Self Help," which supports that same expression, "If it's going to be, it's up to me."

"Self-help or self-improvement refers to self-guided improvement — economically, intellectually, or emotionally —most frequently with a substantial psychological or spiritual basis. The basis for self-help is often self-reliance, publicly available information, or support groups where people in similar situations join together." (Retrieved July 7, 2008)

This reminds me of an expression from years ago, "great salespeople don't wait for sales goals to be handed down from the top, they hand them up to the top."

3. Product Development

In business and engineering, new product development (NPD) is the term used to describe the complete process of bringing a new product or service to market. There are two parallel paths involved in the NPD process: one involves idea generation, product design, and detail engineering; the other involves market research and marketing analysis.

One of the steps in the life cycle of a new product is public awareness. Financial advisors often attend product seminar events thinking that they are getting professional and personal development, when really they're just participating in the company's marketing strategy.

These events are valid and useful, as long as advisors do not use them as a replacement for other development and educational activities.

You are uninspired

I often ask groups of financial advisors what inspired them to become financial advisors in the first place.

Almost every one of the respondents speaks about making a difference to someone else. Like this man: "In the beginning, it was to make money and build a practice. But after my wife was stricken with a critical illness, I now still want to make money and build a successful practice, but really have a passion to help people so they can be safe when uncontrollable events happen, and to help prepare people to spend their savings in their retirement."

Can you find your original inspiration? Can you look around at your own life and find a new one? Can you borrow inspiration from this advisor or a similar story that you have heard?

You are a financial frog

In his Oscar-winning documentary, Al Gore tries to wake us up to the facts about just how much damage we have done and are continuing to do to the earth. He compares us to the frog who sits passively in a pot full of water as it gradually heats up and then boils him to death.

Well, a financial advisor with the *Unmet Needs Disease* is just like that frog. You are sitting passively while your *Unmet Needs* boil up and kill any chance you have for lasting success.

You are a financial monkey with an ulcer

Take a look at the following thought experiment.

One hundred monkeys are divided into four groups:

- The first group of monkeys receives electric shocks at regular intervals and develops ulcers in 24 days.
- The second group of monkeys receives shocks at random intervals. They develop ulcers in 10 days.
- The third group of monkeys has shocks at regular intervals and they have a shock avoidance button. If they time it right, they can avoid the shock. This group develops ulcers in 8 days.
- The fourth group of monkeys gets shocks at random intervals and has a shock avoidance button. These monkeys develop ulcers in only 3 days.

Financial advisors with *Unmet Needs Disease* are like the fourth group of monkeys. You think you can avoid a financial shock but you really have no idea when it is coming. Playing this game only fuels your addiction to adrenaline and keeps you busy so you can avoid reality.

However, you can do better than a simple shock avoidance button. You can have an up-to-date Budget Cash Flow Spreadsheet that will project your monthly bank balance for the next twelve months.

This spreadsheet will start with your opening bank balances, and then:

- Subtract any checks that have not cleared
- Subtract any loans payments
- Subtract any tax contributions
- Subtract any expected expenses

- Add your actual income from consulting and products
- Add projected income from consulting and products

You are left with a projected bank balance for the month.

Not having an up-to-date Budget Cash Flow Spreadsheet fuels your negative ego mind's focus on the *Unmet Need* for safety. This leads to the incapacitating negative emotions of anxiety and fear and contributes to the negative beliefs and the perpetuated false reality that, "money is tight."

Once I have taught them how to use this planning tool, I've seen financial advisors go from uncertainty about the future and having negative beliefs, to having increased clarity and excitement about the future.

It's so ironic. The negative ego mind fools you into thinking that you have no time to plan, that you have to keep doing and doing and doing because you don't have enough money and time. When, in fact, not knowing these bank balances creates more anxiety about the future.

Most of my clients are pleasantly surprised to see how their numbers look. When they finally take charge and face the fear of their negative ego mind, the bottom line is often times better than they expected.

How would you approach your day if your bottom line was better than you expected? Put away the antacids, get your head out of the sand, and stop those shocks before they happen.

You are addicted to selling

In the Clear Values Scorecard, I asked where you are on the continuum between, "I lack focus," and, "I follow a written 5-year vision and business plan." You know what? The answer is yes or no; you are either a 10 or a 1. There is no maybe in the middle.

At the Advisors Forum Conference in Toronto in December 2004, an industry expert speaker said that most advisors are not interested in building their business. They're addicted to selling. That probably explains why 33% of advisors do not have a written vision or business plan.

What's going on?

One explanation is, your negative ego mind says, "Is that all there is?" You are chasing after sales and money because you think they will bring you fulfillment. But, they don't, so the chase continues.

Another reason is, you are trying to meet your *Unmet Need* for safety from outside instead of inside.

In addition, through all of this, you have become addicted to the adrenalin of the sale, which to some people is as potent as any drug.

We come back now to the definition of motivation: the sense of need, desire and fear. Inspiration fulfills you from the inside out but motivation tries to fulfill you from the outside in. Since it is virtually impossible to be fulfilled from the outside in, you feel empty, even though you appear to have reached a goal.

You hear it all the time, "I'll be happy when I have more time/money/clients/holidays/cars/sex, etc." Meanwhile, as you accumulate more and more, your negative ego mind replies with, "Is that all there is?"

Have you ever woken up, gradually becoming more alert and thinking casually about the day ahead, and then bang, it hits you. "Holy shit! I quit the perfectly good job that my mother told me to keep and became a financial advisor, an entrepreneur, and started my own business!"

Having no guaranteed paycheck fuels your *Unmet Need* for safety. So, without really knowing it, you look to your clients and your sales to fulfill your *Unmet Need* and to take care of you. Instead of going out and adding 100% value to your clients, you are looking for them to save you.

You run after any prospect that could fog a mirror and as you approach each one, you think, "Please buy my product, I really need this sale!" This continuing pattern of emotional highs and lows perpetuates the vicious cycle of your adrenalin addiction.

Obsessive Compulsive Product Disorder

The January 16th 2006 edition of Time Magazine has a fantastic article by Claudia Wallis, "Help! I've lost my focus." It's about people who have trouble staying focused at work.

In the article, attention-deficit disorder (ADD) specialist Dr. Edward Hallowell, coins a new term: attention-deficit trait (ADT), for people who have trouble staying focused only in certain situations like work. If you suspect you might suffer from this trait, read the article by visiting www.time.com and typing the article title into the search box.

I've coined my own term - Obsessive Compulsive Product Disorder (OCPD). Advisors with OCPD have no vision or focus, so they are driven by flavor-of-the-month products. They're addicted to the sale (see the previous symptom) and will do anything to get it, expecting their clients to fulfill their *Unmet Needs.*

Wise and well-meaning niche marketing specialists have made the rounds and most financial advisors have started to get the message that specialization is a key element of success. They want to brand themselves like the big guys do, and they know they need a hook.

They're right, but this one step won't work by itself. For an advisor with OCPD, the day might go like this: At an 8:00 a.m. appointment, they sell some critical illness. This gives them the idea to specialize in critical illness. Then at 10:00 a.m., they have another appointment and they sell some life insurance. Now it's to heck with critical illness, they're going to become known far and wide as the life insurance expert.

At a luncheon appointment, they sell some group insurance. Now, that's the ticket! At the end of the day, after they sell some disability insurance, all of a sudden they do not know where to focus. They're running around in circles.

You see, it is impossible to apply branding, niche marketing and product specialization without a strong foundation of values and vision for you and your business to stand on. Otherwise, you will keep grabbing at every new potential niche that pops up in front of you.

You call your clients, "Sir"

Does it make you wary to be called "Sir" by another businessperson? When a client recently called me "Sir," I told him straight out that it was not necessary, "Simon is just fine, thanks."

Advisors who address their clients as "Sir" are reaching out for the acceptance and respect they did not receive in their childhood.

In my client's case, he went through years of university to follow the traditional career path of his family, and gain their acceptance and respect. At the end of it all, he graduated and there was no pot of gold like the one his negative ego mind had him chasing after. No automatic approval from his family, and so, he chose a different career path entirely.

Though he finished his degree, he's still dealing with the unfinished business of his *Unmet Needs* of acceptance and respect.

If your negative ego is subconsciously trying to meet the *Unmet Needs* of acceptance and respect, it is generating the negative beliefs that, "people don't accept me," and "people don't respect me."

Worse yet, the harder you try to get it, the more people you attract who don't fulfill their end of the bargain. We attract what we believe.

Even I had a role in this play. By pointing out some of the actions that my client committed to but didn't follow through on, in essence, my client's negative ego mind heard that I didn't accept or respect him. That further triggered his *Unmet Needs*, negative emotions and beliefs. Even though I was trying to help my client, all his negative ego mind heard was a reminder of the many times in the past when he didn't feel accepted and respected.

Calling someone "Sir" is an expression of a patriarchal dynamic and usually a subconscious attempt to replay a childhood scene, but with a better outcome; finally being told you are good enough, to repair the damage of all of those times being told you weren't.

This brings me back to one of the few times my father spent with me outside of his own busy work schedule. I was seven years old, and was taking swimming lessons at a local pool. My father took me to the lake one Sunday to give me more practice. I can still remember his words, "Look at how well those kids can swim!"

At the time, I didn't know my father never got the approval he needed from his own parents. He was just acting out what he knew, but I called out in self-defense and hurt, "But Dad, those boys are twelve-years-old; they are twice as old as me."

How many times in the next 10 to 20 years will my client run into people and situations that will continue to remind him of not being accepted and respected? What will it cost him to not address this issue? I hope that he lets me help him to turn these 10 to 20 years of unnecessary struggle into years of success.

You don't know when to quit

In his book, *The Dip*, Seth Godin writes about quitting the things that do not give you joy, the wrong stuff. Outsource them, he says, stick with the right stuff and be the best in your world at that. Have the guts to do one or the other.

You have to quit regularly in order to grow. We fail when we get distracted by tasks that we didn't have the guts to quit.

Why don't we have the guts to quit? Because we have the *Unmet Need* for safety. Playing it safe allows you to be ordinary and blameless. However, average, mediocre and ordinary are not good enough. If you are not going to do what it takes to be the best in the world, why bother? Coping is a lousy alternative to quitting.

Compliance problems and rogue behavior

Jennifer McLaughlin wrote a feature for the Compliance Check section of the December 2001 issue of Advisor's Edge magazine about "rogue advisors" and their impact on the industry.

Regulatory associations were contemplating making it mandatory for dealer firms to report complaints to the associations, and publicly document any disciplinary actions against financial advisors.

The article noted that for advisors, unfortunately, emphasis is placed more upon performance (which we know is based on *Unmet Needs* and the motivation to get them met from the outside) than on superb service (which we know is based on values and the inspiration to express them from the inside).

Individuals who perform well can be given a great deal of slack, and that may lead to temptation to act in questionable ways. This rogue behavior is always an expression of *Unmet Needs*, most likely for recognition, achievement, approval, control, respect and/or security.

The strong motivation to get these needs met can lead to compliance problems and conflict of interest. Integrity and service take a back seat to praise and sales.

Financial advisors have a responsibility to provide their clients with recommendations only for investments that are suitable for them. An *Unmet Need* for approval though, overrides or dominates the financial advisor's judgment. If an advisor has a personal interest in a certain area, such as tech stocks, he may subconsciously or even consciously try to sway all of his clients to purchase these products so he can live out his self-perception as an expert and get the approval and accolades he is craving.

It takes time and effort to keep up with current regulations and keep track of changes to your clients' status. If an advisor is dealing with an insatiable *Unmet Need* for achievement, he may act first and check later, and compliance problems occur.

One of the biggest mistakes a financial advisor can make is to assume that because a client talks aggressively about investments, that he actually is aggressive.

The client may be expressing his own *Unmet Needs* of security with this aggressive language. If a client is making quick decisions that you think are wrong, consider parting ways.

When you and your client disagree about the best action, watch out for your *Unmet Need* for control. It can lead to rogue behavior such as signing on behalf of your client or filling in forms without the client being present. It's not about whether your way is right or better. It's about working with integrity, complying with industry regulations and providing the superb customer service that will grow your business.

Only an advisor who has conquered his *Unmet Needs* can have the courage to let a client go when it's not working out and be professional enough to always comply with industry regulations.

Not staying in touch with clients

The number one reason clients give when asked why they left an advisor is lack of contact and the number one reason that advisors do not stay in touch with their clients is the *Unmet Needs Disease.*

The *Unmet Need* for recognition leads advisors to want to get as many clients as possible. That way, they can say to their colleagues and families, "Look at how many clients I've got!" The *Unmet Need* for approval leads advisors to over-promise to their prospective clients, saying anything to get them to sign on.

The *Unmet Need* for safety creates a cycle of overwork, inefficiency and the continuous drive to get more clients. That leaves advisors too busy to serve their existing clients properly. The thrill of chasing a potential new client is more exciting than carrying out the work to service an actual client, so the adrenalin addiction is also triggered.

When an advisor sees he's not providing the service he promised, he feels guilty and the *Unmet Need* for approval kicks up again. Therefore, he avoids the client and doesn't take any action. When the client (inevitably) leaves, it reinforces the advisor's *Unmet Need* for worth and the negative belief that, "I am not good enough." To quickly cover this up, the advisor scrambles to get more clients and the entire process repeats itself. He's on a hamster wheel and he doesn't even know it.

You don't approach high net worth clients

You know the secret to attracting more profitable cases and larger clients but, every time you get close to doing it, you freeze.

You know that you have to segment your clients into four groups: A, B, C & D. Maybe you have even gone to your computer and done it. That's the easy part. And then, you freeze.

The next step is much harder. You have to actually have a conversation with those C and D clients, maybe even the B's. Something like this: "John, I really appreciate working with you. We have a great relationship and I want that relationship to continue. As in most industries, we've got a shortage of financial advisors in my specialty, and so I'm going to be focusing solely on that from now on. That's why I've hired Frank. Frank specializes in the area where you need the most service, and he has the expertise that you need. I'm going to keep an eye on what Frank is doing for you. I want to work with you both on this. Would that be okay with you?"

Sounds easy, so why does it feel so hard?

Some of these clients might be among your earliest, and getting them initially made you feel like you were meeting your *Unmet Needs* of safety and approval. You need to detach from that and realize that no outside source can truly meet your *Unmet Needs*. Servicing these clients is keeping you stuck and blocking you from attracting the bigger and more profitable clients that you want and deserve.

Keep this in mind as well... referrals are like water - they find their own level. If your current clients are at a certain income level, they will likely be referring other clients at that similar level. That is what you have attracted and that is what you will continue to attract, unless you make a change.

I've worked with five-year veterans and thirty-year veterans, and it's the same thing. They hit a ceiling and can't break through. The *Unmet Need* for worthiness is replaying the same negative belief message over and over again, "I am not good enough to work with high net worth clients. I don't know enough and I don't have enough experience." The outcome? No action and no results.

After I've helped advisors cure their *Unmet Needs Disease*, I hear things like, "I don't know what's going on. Prospects I have been calling for ten years are suddenly calling *me*." These financial advisors have strengthened themselves from the inside out. They are no longer trying to prove themselves. They are comfortable, they are centered and interestingly enough, that changes the entire environment around them.

Giving referrals to get something

Not getting enough quality referrals?

Perhaps it is time to look at the referrals you are giving.

Are you giving the referral to "give" or is your negative ego mind giving the referral to "get?"

When you give a referral to give value, it comes from the place of you wanting to add value to both the person that you are giving the referral to and the person you are referring.

You have no other agenda but to provide a boost to both parties.

Have you seen the movie *Pay it Forward*? If you haven't, please put it on your list. In the movie, to pay it forward is to perform acts of unsolicited kindness for three people; with the only expectation being that the recipients will perform their own acts of kindness to three other people.

If your negative ego mind is expressing your *Unmet Needs* for approval, control, perfection, power, recognition, safety and the granddaddy of all *Unmet Needs*, worthiness, then it is likely you have got some expectations of both the people you are giving the referral to and the people you are referring. Your negative ego is giving the referral in order to get something.

Maybe it has to hear, "Wow, thanks, you are the best." or, "Hey, you were right about that guy," or, "You always know the best people."

You might not be asking right out for a commission (don't you just love those?), but if you have an expectation for payback of any kind, it will come across. It will affect how your referrals are received, and it will definitely affect the referrals that you get.

Remember - what goes around, comes around. Give referrals when it adds value to both parties, and that value will come back to you.

When it comes to asking for referrals, it's the same thing. Are you asking your client for a referral to fulfill an *Unmet Need* or are you asking because you want to add value to your client and to the person they will refer you to?

Having the succession conversation too late

This story is a composite of several experiences where a senior advisor with over 25 years of experience brought a novice advisor into their business. It highlights the fact that human beings are basically honest, but at the same time, boundaries are so important.

The senior advisor had a lack of vision, brought on by unresolved *Unmet Needs*, and therefore had weak leadership boundaries with the novice advisor.

Casually over lunch one day, the senior advisor says, "We can talk about being partners one day."

Five years later, the senior and novice advisor finally get around to creating a partnership agreement, and the relationship ends in a heated conflict. You see, both were thinking of a 50/50 split, but they were thinking of it in a very different way.

The senior advisor believes that his business is worth $250K, based on the 25 years he spent building it before the novice advisor arrived. So, he expects the novice to pay him 50% of $250K ($125K).

The novice advisor, fueled by a Generation X/Y sense of entitlement, expects to be handed 50% of the business's earnings. He has no idea of the value of the business when he came in, never mind what it took the senior advisor to build it before he got there.

The novice advisor quickly forgets what it took the senior advisor to build the business, while he slid in front of all of these quality A-clients with zero sweat equity to attract them. After all, anyone can walk out in front of someone's audience (well, almost).

I have seen this same scenario play out more than once, and every time it has ended every time in a shit fight.

The solution:

- Know what your values are (get your *Unmet Needs* identified and met)
- Have a clear vision for the future
- Use a hiring strategy that includes values and behaviors assessments, to weed out takers versus givers

- Have a clear and documented conversation with new associates and employees about the value of the business at their point of entry and the fee if they want to buy in
- Don't use the word partnership with anyone who has been with you in your business for less than 5 years.

Telltale emotions of the Unmet Needs Disease

Most of us have a very limited vocabulary of emotions - we feel good or we feel bad.

Here are some of the negative emotions you may start to identify when you tune into the effects of your *Unmet Needs Disease*:

Afraid, angry, anxious, ashamed, bitter, confused, depressed, disappointed, discouraged, embarrassed, exhausted, fearful, frightened, helpless, hesitant, hurt, impatient, irritated, jealous, listless, lonely, miserable, nervous, overwhelmed, panicky, resentful, sad, scared, terrified, tired, uncomfortable, unhappy, upset, weary, withdrawn and worried.

But, hey, here are some of the positive feelings you may experience once you are expressing your values:

Adventurous, alive, amazed, animated, appreciative, blissful, cheerful, comfortable, confident, delighted, ecstatic, encouraged, energetic, enthusiastic, excited, exhilarated, fascinated, free, fulfilled, gleeful, glorious, grateful, happy, inspired, intrigued, joyful, loving, optimistic, peaceful, pleased, radiant, satisfied, stimulated, thankful, thrilled and wonderful.

"You were absolutely right. I do feel more clear, confident, and more fulfilled - that everything is getting easier. I look forward to our next call."

Edna Keep
Assante Financial Management Ltd.
Regina, SK

Chapter 7:

The Cure

Curing the Unmet Needs Disease is a specific three-part process which we will cover in-depth in the coming pages. Along with that, though, it is a lifelong daily practice of new habits that feed our values and starve our negative ego mind.

You can start that practice right now. The choice is yours.

At Leading Advisor, we have a saying, "The client does the work, the client does the work, the client does the work."

Part 2 of this book is all about the cure, and it's all about work. If you do the work, it will work. If you make time for it, it will work for you.

"Out of all of the coaches that I have worked with, you are the only one that gets it and I received an incredible amount of value in a short period of time."

Brad Gustafson
Partner
Richardson Partners Financial
Calgary, AB

Part 2:

The Cure

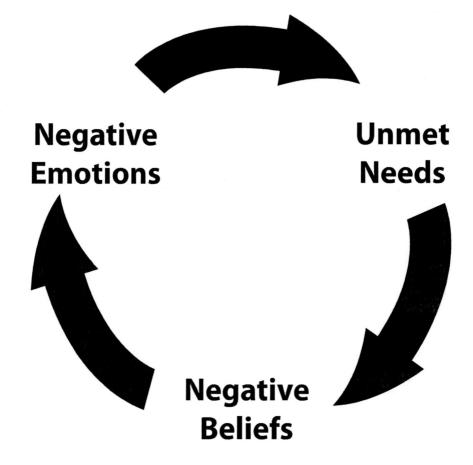

The Clear Your Roadblocks Program

The Clear Your Roadblocks Program is a three-step process to:

1. Clear your *Unmet Needs*
2. Clear your Negative Emotions
3. Clear your Negative Beliefs

The reason for our approach is simple and answers the question why personal development and the Law of Attraction may not have worked for you in the past.

Personal development and the Law of Attraction both focus on having, and working with, positive beliefs.

If you have an *Unmet Need*, you have negative emotions supercharging your negative beliefs. Your *Unmet Need*, negative emotions and negative beliefs undermine any chance for a value, positive feeling or positive belief to manifest.

Chapter 8:
Clear your Unmet Needs

Step 1. – Do you have Unmet Needs?

These are some of the negative emotions that you experience when *Unmet Needs* are not met. How many of them do you experience, and how often?

Negative Emotions

Afraid	Frightened	Panicky
Angry	Helpless	Resentful
Anxious	Hesitant	Sad
Ashamed	Hurt	Scared
Bitter	Impatient	Terrified
Confused	Irritated	Tired
Depressed	Jealous	Uncomfortable
Disappointed	Listless	Unhappy
Discouraged	Lonely	Upset
Embarrassed	Miserable	Weary
Exhausted	Nervous	Withdrawn
Fearful	Overwhelmed	Worried

Wouldn't you rather experience the positive feelings on the next list?

These are some of the positive feelings that you experience when *Unmet Needs* are met and when you are expressing your values. How many of them do you experience, and how often?

Positive Feelings

Adventurous	Energetic	Intrigued
Alive	Enthusiastic	Joyful
Amazed	Excited	Loving
Animated	Exhilarated	Optimistic
Appreciative	Fascinated	Peaceful
Blissful	Free	Pleased
Cheerful	Fulfilled	Radiant
Comfortable	Gleeful	Satisfied
Confident	Glorious	Stimulated
Delighted	Grateful	Thankful
Ecstatic	Happy	Thrilled
Encouraged	Inspired	Wonderful

Step 2. – Why is it important to get your Unmet Needs met?

Financial advisors may "want" a vision and business plan but they hamstring themselves with a lack of focus created by the *Unmet Need* for perfection. Though they come to realize they need a niche and product to build a vision and business plan on, their negative ego sabotages them. The *Unmet Need* for perfection combined with the negative belief of, "it or they may not be good enough," combined with the negative emotion of anxiety, keeps them trying one thing after another, finally overwhelming them.

Financial Advisors may "want" referrals but they hamper themselves with procrastination because of their *Unmet Need* for approval. The majority of financial advisors agree that asking for referrals is the most effective way to build their business, but their negative ego sabotages them here again. The *Unmet Need* for approval, combines with the negative belief of "I may make a mistake," and with the negative emotion of fear, and even though they may struggle through their fear to ask for a referral, their fear-based energy is picked up by the client and the client says, "No."

The point is, you know what you need to do. You might even be baffled by why you are not doing it. It's simple. You have *Unmet Needs*.

Step 3. – Survivors vs. Advisors

Let's review the Clear Values Scorecard.

The Clear Values Scorecard.

	Financial Survivor	Financial Advisor
1	I lack focus.	I follow a written 5-year vision and business plan.
2	I am not making as much money as I would like.	I am fully satisfied with the amount of money I am making.
3	I have to get myself pumped when I am selling.	I feel naturally excited about my work and I enjoy the selling process.
4	I feel I am not getting enough referrals.	I am getting many great, qualified referrals.
5	I feel that I am working too hard, with too many unqualified or C and D clients.	I am getting many new high-quality clients.

6	I try to serve anyone and everyone.	I have branded my business and I am focused on a niche market.
7	I do too many favors and I sell too many products.	I am focused on profitable products and services.
8	I feel completely overwhelmed, doing things I don't like to do.	I do what I love to do and have a hiring system to delegate everything else.
9	I have a lot of conflict in my business relationships.	I manage my business relationships extremely well.
10	I beat myself up when things don't go right and I have lost my enthusiasm for my business.	I always celebrate my successes and learn from my setbacks. I am achieving my true potential as an advisor.

Which one are you?

- The financial survivor who needs a client, or the financial advisor who adds value to a client?
- The financial survivor who is looking for motivation, or the financial advisor who works from inspiration?
- The financial survivor who is stuck, or the financial advisor who is evolved?
- The financial survivor who does, or the financial advisor who delegates?
- The financial survivor who works not to lose the client, or the financial advisor who works to serve the client and grow the client's assets?
- The financial survivor who oversells, or the financial advisor who undersells?
- The financial survivor who overpromises, or the financial advisor who over-delivers?
- The financial survivor who is conflicted, or the financial advisor who is in harmony?

- The financial survivor who is emotionally retired, or the financial advisor who is enthusiastic?

Please note that some of the concepts above were developed from the theory of "Irresistible Attraction" by the late Thomas Leonard, founder of Coach U.

Step 4. – Identify your Unmet Needs

Here is a list of typical *Unmet Needs*:

- Acceptance
- Accomplishment
- Achievement
- Acknowledgement
- Admired
- Appreciation
- Approval
- Attention
- Certainty
- Confident
- Control
- Heard
- Helpful
- Honored
- Importance
- Included
- Independence
- Listened To
- Noticed
- Perfection
- Please
- Power
- Prove

- Recognition
- Respect
- Safety
- Security
- Thanked
- Trusted
- Understood
- Worthiness

Here are some specific *Unmet Needs* that may lead to lower scores on The Clear Values Scorecard.

	Financial Survivor	Possible *Unmet Needs*
1	I lack focus.	Perfection
2	I am not making as much money as I would like.	Safety
3	I have to get myself pumped when I am selling.	Recognition
4	I feel I am not getting enough referrals.	Approval
5	I feel that I am working too hard, with too many unqualified or C and D clients.	Appreciation
6	I try to serve anyone and everyone.	Respect
7	I do too many favors and I sell too many products.	To Please
8	I feel completely overwhelmed, doing things I don't like to do.	Control
9	I have a lot of conflict in my business relationships.	Power
10	I beat myself up when things don't go right and I have lost my enthusiasm for my business.	Worthiness

Read through the previous list of *Unmet Needs* again and circle the ones you can identify with.

You might want to set the list aside for a while before the next step.

When you come back to the list, out of the ones you circled, star (*) the four *Unmet Needs* that are the strongest. Finally, identify the number one *Unmet Need* that speaks to you.

As an example, one could have the following four *Unmet Needs* circled:

- Achievement
- Approval
- Safety
- Worthiness

Perhaps you chose achievement as your number one *Unmet Need.*

Not so fast.

Ask yourself, can you achieve when those other three *Unmet Needs*, negative beliefs and negative emotions are all still working against you? Remember, we're talking about:

Unmet Needs	Negative Emotions	Negative Beliefs
Approval	Sadness	People don't appreciate what I do for them
Safety	Anxiety	I don't have enough money or time.

Worthiness	Despair	Nothing I do is good enough.

Could you achieve with all of that going on?

No.

Even worse, through the Law of Attraction you continue to attract the negative evidence that makes the *Unmet Needs* and negative beliefs and negative emotions real. Whether you believe in the Law of Attraction or not, you are attracting something. The question is, what are you attracting?

To choose the deepest or strongest *Unmet Need*, ask yourself which *Unmet Need* you have to meet first because without doing so, you will not be able to meet the others.

Step 5. – Understand the origin of your Unmet Need

With your number one *Unmet Need* in mind, write a story that starts out with "when I was a little boy or girl…" and think back as far as you can remember to a time when you first experienced your *Unmet Need*.

Your story doesn't need to be about a cataclysmic event. *Unmet Needs* are actually quite simple in a child's mind.

As you tell the story, include how you felt, e.g., rejected, angry, sad, worthless. Please refer to the Negative Emotions List in Chapter 8, Step 1.

For me, one of my *Unmet Needs* was approval and here is my story…

When I was a little boy, I was running home with a straight-A report card. It was a beautiful spring day with blue skies and white billowy cumulous clouds back dropping blooming pink cherry tree blossoms. As I ran, I noticed I could run faster than ever before, almost running right over top of the gangly legs I had sprouted over the winter months. I ran across the lawn calling, "Dad, Dad... look, I got a straight-A report card!" And then, my Dad said, "But you got a B in Art."

I felt the following negative emotions: angry, ashamed, bitter, dejected, disappointed, hurt, irritated, rejected, resentful, and unhappy.

Little did I know that my father had the same unresolved and incomplete *Unmet Need* for approval; how could he give me something he didn't have?

As a result of my *Unmet Need* for approval and those negative emotions, I started a series of lifelong imbedded negative beliefs that included:

- I am not good enough
- Nothing I ever do is good enough
- My father doesn't love me

And, the granddaddy of them all...

- I hate my father

Whew! That was it, now I'd done it. I felt so bad. Now I felt guilty too. How would I ever earn back the love of my father?

I went to work, giving and giving and giving, all the while trying to get my *Unmet Need* met from outside of myself. I tried to gain the approval and resulting love of my father, which could never happen because of his own *Unmet Need*.

Even worse, through the Law of Attraction I continued to attract the negative evidence that made the *Unmet Need* and negative emotions and negative beliefs real.

I attached these limiting emotions and negative beliefs to people who could never satisfy my *Unmet Need* for approval, and time and again, I came to the conclusion of another negative belief: people only take and take and take and I feel so angry.

Little did I know that like attracts like. I was attracting negative circumstances and people that were a reflection of my *Unmet Needs*, negative beliefs and negative emotions.

An *Unmet Need* cannot be met through an accomplishment, money, person, possession, position or relationship. No *thing* will ever meet the *Unmet Need* from outside of the self, it must be met from within using the following process.

Step 6. - Clear your Unmet Needs

Use a journal to write out the following exercises. Thinking them through doesn't count.

Write a list of 10 simple actions you can do to take care of yourself.

Borrow from the list below or add your own. Don't include any actions that involve another person, except for professionals such as massage therapists or coaches.

Talking to friends and family doesn't get your needs met. Your *Unmet Need* <u>must</u> be met from within. As an adult, trying to get your *Unmet Needs* met through family and friends can lead to co-dependency issues.

Notice that our sample list does not include:
- Answer email
- Surf the Net
- Go to a party
- Talk on the phone
- Text messaging
- Listening to my iPod

You cannot clear your *Unmet Needs* by buying things or socializing.

10 simple actions that make you feel safe and taken care of:
- Do my nails
- Drink a glass of water
- Get a therapeutic massage

- Listen to inspirational music
- Read inspirational books
- Stand or sit in the sunshine for a few minutes
- Take a deep breath
- Take vitamins
- Walk in nature
- Write in my journal

1. _____
2. _____
3. _____
4. _____
5. _____
6. _____
7. _____
8. _____
9. _____
10. _____

For each action, write about how to clear your *Unmet Need* (using safety as an example) and how that makes you feel, by filling in this sentence:

I observe my *Unmet Need* for safety being cleared whenever I _____ and therefore I feel _____.

Please refer to the Positive Feelings List in Chapter 8, Step 1.

These simple affirmations, combined with the actions you do for yourself will clear and complete your *Unmet Needs* from within.

Your obsessive negative ego mind will slow down; you will have less busyness and you will be able to relax. In the process, you will be a lot more attractive to more qualified business with less effort.

Come back to this exercise again to work through each of your *Unmet Needs* as a daily practice. It may take anywhere from one to three years to meet all of your *Unmet Needs*.

Here is a story of how one of my clients worked to clear his *Unmet Needs*.

Dick's story – playing with fire

Dick was a seasoned veteran with two and a half decades in the insurance industry; his sales records were legendary.

Dick was so driven to achieve his income goals, he had little time for people or idle chitchat. "Time is money," after all. He felt like he was on fire, but he was oblivious to the effects that his fire-driven personality was having on those around him.

His associates, team members and even his clients all found him to be too abrupt and pushy. They stayed with him because he offered the best prices on his products and he made himself available 24/7 via cell phone.

His self-righteous and unbending rules were difficult to follow, and eventually even the best assistant could not satisfy him. This was a reflection of Dick's negative ego mind's negative belief that, "nothing is good enough."

Needless to say, Dick could not keep assistants. His last assistant experienced so much discomfort, she quit by leaving a letter of resignation on his desk over the weekend, being too afraid to resign in person.

His personal life was a mess as well. His weekly routine usually involved a debate with at least one of his ex-wives over child support, and he felt that he could never give them enough to keep them satisfied.

While he was like a bull in a china shop, Dick had a soft center and he really just wanted people to like him.

At the same time, he had an insatiable need for safety. Dick had one of those t-shirts that read, "The one that dies with the most toys wins." He had the marble counter tops, the in-home media centre and spa and a Lexus in the driveway. But, no matter how much he sold, and how much he bought, none of it was ever enough.

His quest to attain new things and take care of the things he had, left him with very little quiet time. His mind was preoccupied with an obsession to land "the big fish." However, even though high net worth clients were willing to listen to his spiel, they were really looking for someone who was more grounded. They saw that he could not keep staff over the long term and that did not make a good impression.

Failing to close a case gave Dick's ego the ammunition to hammer him with the negative beliefs that, "Nothing I do is good enough," and "No matter how hard I try I can never seem to close the big case." These negative beliefs were a self-fulfilling prophecy, and Dick just kept trying even harder.

Being a veteran in sales, Dick had been to many of the self-help and sales seminars but nothing seemed to work. He was at his wits end and he had to do something fast.

Some said he was like an accident waiting to happen. It happened.

Life is about messages. If you get the message, you get an attainment and move on to the next level. If you don't get the message, you'll create a problem. If you don't fix the problem, then you'll create a crisis. Then, hopefully, you'll get the message.

On his way to a sales appointment, Dick was driving far too fast on wet slippery roads. Not only did he miss the appointment, he rolled his Lexus. An old-timer who ran up to his car to see if he was okay saw Dick pull himself out of the overturned car and exclaimed, "You must have horse shoes up yer arse."

That accident was the wake-up call that Dick needed. The next call he made was to me.

The first thing I had Dick do in our work together was to clear his *Unmet Needs*.

While he always felt there was something more important to do, he made a decision to wake up a little earlier each morning to write in his journal.

Here is a sample of journalings that he used to clear his *Unmet Needs;*

- I observe my *Unmet Need* for safety being cleared whenever I take time for myself and therefore I feel appreciative.
- I observe my *Unmet Need* for safety being cleared whenever I journal and therefore I feel more satisfied.
- I observe my *Unmet Need* for safety being cleared whenever I experience the environment when I am walking and therefore I feel thankful.

Dick also made it a habit to write in his journal each week about all of the accomplishments in his business and personal life, both large and small.

Adopting this new practice took Dick a little while. However, even while his negative ego mind was grumbling, "Why do I have to do this touchy feely shit," for some reason he started to feel more settled.

It did not happen right away, like going to a motivational seminar and feeling like you are being shot out of a cannon. This was different.

After a few days of using his journal to clear his *Unmet Needs*, he caught himself walking down the street feeling happier and asked himself, "Why do I feel so good?" It dawned on him that the simple little journaling process was causing him to take the time for himself and give him the self-love that he needed.

Dick became more aware of the abundance in his life, and that the present moment was perfect. Now, he had far less worry about the future.

He began meeting with his assistant on a regular basis instead of hurling her things to do without being clear about priorities.

These regular meetings began by stating one or two things he noticed that the assistant was doing really well. This long-forgotten idea from Ken Blanchard's book, *The One Minute Manager,* came back to him while he was writing in his journal.

Given that Dick was now taking more time for himself, he also found time to create a prioritized project list for his assistant and reviewed it with her during their meetings. Together, they came up with the highest priorities. The assistant felt more like a team member and less like a thing.

As Dick cleared his *Unmet Needs*, he began to reflect on his story. He looked for what it was about his past that made him so impatient, and what had him believing that he didn't have enough and that he wasn't good enough.

Chapter 9:

Clear your Negative Emotions

Find a quiet place with your journal, preferably in a natural setting where you can connect with the elements - air, earth, fire and water. If you can't find such a place, go where you can be alone and anonymous. Sometimes you can be alone and anonymous at a coffee shop that you don't frequent. Go to the library. You can even rent a boardroom in an office.

With your story in mind, be open to any other memories or thoughts that may come to you during this process. Jot it down in the margin of your page. You can come back to it later to write out that story, the negative emotions and the negative beliefs.

For some people, right about now, their negative ego mind is yelling, "Red alert!" The last thing it wants is for you to be alone with your emotions. After all, the negative ego mind has kept you running your entire life trying to avoid your negative emotions. You may have heard that, "What you resist, persists," "Whatever you defend against, you make real," and, "Whatever you don't clean up in one relationship you bring it to the next, only ten times worse."

The negative ego mind tries to protect you from these negative emotions by saying, "It's time to get busy! What's on CNN? You'd better check your Blackberry, you might be missing something!"

It is time for you to take charge of your fear-based negative ego mind to demonstrate that these fears are unreal. Nothing outside of you exists until you choose to feel and believe the experience. You are the creator of your experience.

You are not your negative ego mind. You are a being, a soul; however, you care to describe it.

You are missing something, but it clearly won't be found on CNN or your Blackberry. This is your opportunity to clear your roadblocks from the inside out. Do whatever it takes to find a place to be still, and clear your negative emotions and negative beliefs.

One last thing to remember before we begin: this process is intended for your private use and it is not recommended that you share your work with anyone because they may not understand this process and they could take it personally.

To clear your negative emotions, you are going to write about them in this three-step process:

1. I am feeling ...
2. Forgive me for feeling ...
3. Forgive me for forgetting ...

Step 1. – Identify your negative emotions

Review your story and circle all the negative emotions. Go ahead, tell the truth about how you are feeling and let it all hang out. List as many of your negative emotions as you can. Have you got 15? 20? The more, the better.

Getting back to my story

When I was a little boy, I was running home with a straight-A report card. It was a beautiful spring day with blue skies and white billowy cumulous clouds back dropping blooming pink cherry tree blossoms. As I ran, I noticed I could run faster than ever before, almost running right over top of the gangly legs I had sprouted over the winter months. I ran across the lawn calling, "Dad, Dad... look, I got a straight-A report card!" And then, my Dad said, "But you got a B in Art."

I felt the following negative emotions: angry, ashamed, bitter, dejected, disappointed, hurt, irritated, rejected, resentful, and unhappy.

Now that you have your list of emotions, create a space for the three-step process by preparing your page like this:

Step 1 _____

Step 2 _____

Step 3 _____

* * *

Step 1 _____

Step 2 _____

Step 3 _____

* * *

Step 1 _____

Step 2 _____

Step 3 _____

And so on.

Next, fill in "Step 1" for each emotion, like this:

Step 1   I feel angry

Step 2 _____

Step 3 _____

* * *

Step 1   I feel ashamed

Step 2 _____

Step 3 _____

* * *

Step 1   I feel bitter

Step 2 _____

Step 3 _____

And so on.

The idea here is that you, the being or the soul, are sitting your inner child self or negative ego mind down on your knee and offering the compassion and understanding that your parents didn't have the experience or training to provide, back when your story was first created.

Let's be honest. There are probably things going on in your business and personal lives that generate negative emotions and negative beliefs not unlike the ones from my story.

Negative emotions:

- Angry
- Ashamed
- Bitter
- Dejected
- Disappointed
- Hurt
- Irritated
- Rejected
- Resentful
- Unhappy

Negative beliefs:

- I am not good enough
- Nothing I ever do is good enough

- My father doesn't love me
- I hate my father
- People only take and take and take and I feel so angry.

These are like skeletons in the closet. If you are like me in my past, you have been trying to keep shoving them in there and keep them there, until it took more energy than you had to give.

Once in a while, they all came tumbling out. Sometimes it was when I was on my own, but sometimes when there were other people around - this was disastrous. Having a strong emotion in front of someone else was unbearable and I thought it meant I was broken.

Now I know that only by getting into the deep end of your negative emotions can you increase your capacity for positive emotions and attract what you want in your life in the process. Once you get these negative emotions out of the way, you can think clearly. You will have a deeper compassion and understanding for what is really going on.

Imagine that back in the time of your story, you had maturity beyond your years; you even had a PhD in this process to clear *Unmet Needs*, negative emotions and negative beliefs. In my case, I could have said:

"It's okay that my father can't acknowledge me right now. He's likely having a bad day and doesn't feel appreciated for what he is doing. It's not a good time to share my excitement about my report card. I'll come back at another time when Dad is feeling more resourceful. At the same time, maybe Dad will come to me when he is feeling more resourceful."

If thoughts are real forces (and we know that they are), imagine the reality I could have created with those positive and understanding thoughts.

As you use this process to write about the emotions you have been carrying around in your body for so long, they will literally flow away from you – through your arms, hands, fingers, and right onto the page.

To further clear, some say it is even a good idea to burn the pages after you are through - but not yet, there is still more to do.

So now, you have written out the first step for all of your emotions, like this:

Step 1   I feel angry

Step 2 _____

Step 3 _____

* * *

Step 1   I feel ashamed

Step 2 _____

Step 3 _____

* * *

Step 1   I feel bitter

Step 2 _____

Step 3 _____

* * *

Step 1   I feel dejected

Step 2 _____

Step 3 _____

* * *

Step 1   I feel disappointed

Step 2 _____

Step 3 _____

* * *

Step 1   I feel hurt

Step 2 _____

Step 3 _____

* * *

Step 1   I feel irritated

Step 2 _____

Step 3 _____

* * *

Step 1   I feel rejected

Step 2 _____

Step 3 _____

* * *

Step 1   I feel resentful

Step 2 _____

Step 3 _____

* * *

Step 1   I feel unhappy

Step 2 _____

Step 3 _____

Don't let your negative ego mind get in the way.

Remember, your negative ego mind is on red alert and wants you to run away from these negative emotions. There is an expression that God doesn't give us anything that we can't handle. You can handle this.

Furthermore, there is nothing more important in your business than getting this work completed as soon as possible.

So go ahead, feel the negative emotion and notice that while it is strong, it gets to a point where it doesn't get any stronger... it just is. It has a beginning, middle and end.

Now, you can sit back and observe, "So this is what angry, ashamed, bitter, dejected, disappointed, hurt, irritated, rejected, resentful, and unhappy all feel like."

I like to invite my negative ego mind into an imaginary cave and say, "You have been distracting me with these negative emotions. Let's get into them together and really feel it. Let's get to the bottom of this." The negative ego mind had me believing I could not handle these negative emotions so I better keep running and doing. Now, my true self, being, or soul is offering the compassion, understanding and consciousness to demonstrate that when I sit with the negative emotions and breathe them out, they start to subside and go away.

Go ahead and breathe, I'll bet you are feeling lighter already.

We are ready for the second step to clear your emotions.

Step 2. – Forgiveness

Someone once said that when we forgive, we get back some of the energy that was available to us when we were created.

When we forgive a negative emotion, we neutralize it.

"God's place is all around us, it is in everything and in anything we can experience. People just need to change the way they look at things... when you forgive, you love. And when you forgive, God's light shines through you."

from the movie,
Into the Wild,
Screenplay by Sean Penn

This brings us right back to the Law of Attraction. We attract whatever we are thinking.

There is no benefit to you to attract these negative emotions; angry, ashamed, bitter, dejected, disappointed, hurt, irritated, rejected, resentful, and unhappy. The negative ego mind, however, literally feeds off the negative energy and attracts more of it. It is addicted to this negative energy, to being right about what is wrong.

Before you go onto Step 2, make sure you have listed absolutely all of the negative emotions you can think of in Step 1. If you are ready to proceed, fill in Step 2 like this:

Step 1 I feel angry

Step 2 Forgive me for feeling angry

Step 3 _____

* * *

Step 1 I feel ashamed

Step 2 Forgive me for feeling ashamed

Step 3 _____

* * *

Step 1   I feel bitter

Step 2   Forgive me for feeling bitter

Step 3 _____

* * *

Step 1   I feel dejected

Step 2   Forgive me for feeling dejected

Step 3 _____

* * *

Step 1   I feel disappointed

Step 2   Forgive me for feeling disappointed

Step 3 _____

* * *

Step 1   I feel hurt

Step 2   Forgive me for feeling hurt

Step 3 _____

* * *

Step 1   I feel irritated

Step 2   Forgive me for feeling irritated

Step 3 _____

* * *

Step 1   I feel rejected

Step 2   Forgive me for feeling rejected

Step 3 _____

* * *

Step 1   I feel resentful

Step 2   Forgive me for feeling resentful

Step 3 _____

* * *

Step 1   I feel unhappy

Step 2   Forgive me for feeling unhappy

Step 3 _____

It may seem like you are just repeating Step 1, but note that this is a very important step for neutralizing the emotion and evoking the Law of Attraction. Forgiveness is a very powerful thing.

Just by reading this, you should be starting to feel better, but remember our sayings, "The client does the work, the client does the work, the client does the work," and "If it's going to be, it's up to me."

Hear and you forget; see and you remember;
do and you understand.
Confucius

This is not one of those times to fake it, even if you have been faking it your whole life. Now is the time to get it done.

We are ready for the third step to clear your emotions.

Step 3. – Create positive feelings

Now that you have cleared your emotions, it is time for you to become an alchemist. You have the ability to turn lead into gold, given the Law of Attraction and that, "thoughts are real forces." You now have the opportunity to create a brand-new set of positive feelings. Look back to the Positive Feelings List in Chapter 8, Step 1 for a list of the positive feelings that occur when *Unmet Needs* are met.

Look for emotions that are most related to the negative ones you have listed – the one you think you'd most likely feel if this *Unmet Need* was met.

The main thing to understand about Step 3 is that you are sending out a new vibration.

Step 1 I feel angry

Step 2 Forgive me for feeling angry

Step 3 Forgive me for forgetting I am feeling alive

* * *

Step 1 I feel ashamed

Step 2 Forgive me for feeling ashamed

Step 3 Forgive me for forgetting I am feeling confident

* * *

Step 1 I feel bitter

Step 2 Forgive me for feeling bitter

Step 3 Forgive me for forgetting I am feeling energetic

* * *

Step 1 I feel dejected

Step 2 Forgive me for feeling dejected

Step 3 Forgive me for forgetting I am feeling excited

* * *

Step 1 I feel disappointed

Step 2 Forgive me for feeling disappointed

Step 3 Forgive me for forgetting I am feeling fulfilled

* * *

Step 1 I feel hurt

Step 2 Forgive me for feeling hurt

Step 3 Forgive me for forgetting I am feeling grateful

* * *

Step 1 I feel irritated

Step 2 Forgive me for feeling irritated

Step 3 Forgive me for forgetting I am feeling happy

* * *

Step 1 I feel rejected

Step 2 Forgive me for feeling rejected

Step 3 Forgive me for forgetting I am feeling inspired

* * *

Step 1 I feel resentful

Step 2 Forgive me for feeling resentful

Step 3 Forgive me for forgetting I am feeling satisfied

* * *

Step 1 I feel unhappy

Step 2 Forgive me for feeling unhappy

Step 3 Forgive me for forgetting I am feeling wonderful

Jane's story – feeling rejected and afraid to change

Jane grew up on a small family farm at the edge of town. Her mother and father were older than the parents of the other kids. The youngest of three children, she was considered a mistake. Her two brothers were much older and had already left home for the bright lights of the city by the time Jane was born.

It was no surprise that her brothers had little interest in carrying on the family business. Jane's father was an angry man who drank from time to time.

As Jane approached Grade 5, she noticed that other children's fathers were more active in their lives than hers was. They came to sports events and attended the school plays. Jane's father was always working and she even had to find her own way to school. The farm wasn't on the bus route and her mother didn't drive.

One day, she brought home a beautifully decorated book that she made as a school project. It earned her an A+, and she gleefully presented it to her parents.

Her mother was proud of her and told her so, but that was soon obliterated by this comment from her father, "What's the point in educating girls, their place is on the farm. This is just a waste of time and money." Jane could not understand why she could not please her father. What was wrong with her?

She felt despair, sadness and rejection and became even more afraid of her father. She retreated and withdrew; one of those children who were seen but not heard. She continued to excel in school, however, still seeking out that approval from her father.

The farm wasn't doing very well. In order to have nice clothes like her classmates, Jane took on a small paper route as well as babysitting jobs for families at the church. She started to become a little entrepreneur.

Her mother came to her and asked her if she could borrow some of the money that she was saving. They had fallen short and needed money for the taxes. She gave her savings to her mother and father, and was never paid back. Jane felt rejected and unloved once more.

Then came the June day when they had to leave the farm and move into a small house in town. Her father had to take a job. He grew even more distant and angry, and the drinking became even worse.

Her mother cried a lot. There was so much pain in that small house that Jane got busier and busier with after-school programs and extra jobs. She vowed she would never go through the anguish of not having enough money and she would never experience what her mother and father were going through. She buried herself in work.

The negative emotions Jane carried away from these early experiences were despair, rejection and sadness. Her deep-rooted fear of change was expressed as dread, anxiety and uncertainty.

When Jane and I met, business was good, but not growing. Some of her clients were getting older and others had moved away. Worst of all, competition was nipping at her heels. She had lost some clients who had been with her for years. Jane could see the writing on the wall. She knew that she did not do something soon to add more new clients and grow her business; her once consistent income would go by the wayside.

She needed to change and set out at the beginning of each week with plans to call her clients to discuss new business opportunities and referrals. No matter how hard she seemed to try, Jane always was caught up in emails, red tape and busy work. She could not even find the time to delegate more of these things to her assistant.

When she did attempt to discuss new business opportunities and referrals with her clients, she just could not get the words past the lump in her throat and the fear in her heart.

Stress about her own business compounded with fears about changes in the company her husband worked for. Bankruptcy rumors were in the wind. With their children in university, they still had some pretty big financial commitments.

After another grueling tax season, bringing files home and working around the clock, Jane finally made the choice to invest in coaching and get some much-needed outside perspective. In our work together, I taught her to clear the negative emotions that were connected to her *Unmet Need* for worthiness and her fear of change.

<u>Worthiness</u>

Step 1 I feel despair

Step 2 Forgive me for feeling despair

Step 3 Forgive me for forgetting I love myself

* * *

Step 1 I feel rejected

Step 2 Forgive me for feeling rejected

Step 3 Forgive me for forgetting I am grateful for the opportunities that I have

* * *

Step 1 I feel sad

Step 2 Forgive me for feeling sad

Step 3 Forgive me for forgetting God has given me many gifts and I feel thankful

Change

Step 1 I feel afraid

Step 2 Forgive me for feeling afraid

Step 3 Forgive me for forgetting I have inner strength

* * *

Step 1 I feel anxious

Step 2 Forgive me for feeling anxious

Step 3 Forgive me for forgetting that I am confident

* * *

Step 1 I feel uncertain

Step 2 Forgive me for feeling uncertain

Step 3 Forgive me for forgetting that I am certain

Jane continued to journal and to practice her work to clear her *Unmet Needs* and emotions. Yes, there was resistance. She found that her negative ego mind would do anything to distract her in order to avoid these negative emotions.

In one respect, her negative ego mind was doing her a favor all those years, keeping her away from the negative emotions. However, by avoiding the negative emotions and keeping them just below the surface, they were triggered at the first sign of trouble. All the times she felt unworthy because of the potential fear of rejection and unsafe because of the potential of change spilled over like dominoes.

Once she realized the origin of her negative emotions and worked to clear them, Jane adopted a new belief. In order for things to change, she must change. She started to take the steps that would get her out from being overwhelmed.

Chapter 10:

Clear your Negative Beliefs

Mike's story - how Mike worked to clear his negative beliefs

Mike was brought into the financial advisor industry by his own financial advisor. He shared his frustration about his sales position in a photocopier business, and his advisor convinced him to come on board with him, claiming he had more clients than he could handle.

That might have been true, but do you think he could get the financial advisor to turn any of them over to him? Even after Mike had been there a year and completed his licensing, he wasn't handed any clients.

They argued about it, and the other advisor insisted that Mike still didn't have enough experience. He certainly didn't have any experience with prospecting – in the photocopier business, he sat in a showroom and the clients came to him.

Mike's money was starting to run out, so he had to do everything he could to create an income. Thank goodness, he had sent personalized thank you notes to all of his clients from the photocopier business. He still had their contact information.

Mike found this trial-by-fire very difficult. He felt cheated by the financial advisor who had brought him into the industry. But he persisted, prospecting all of his clients from the photocopier business – from the biggest to the smallest.

By the beginning of his second year, Mike started to make a decent income, but he was bogged down with an enormous amount of paperwork. He was working day and night to keep up.

He was not getting any of the support or any of the clients that the financial advisor had promised him; all he got was a desk and a phone. When Mike finally demanded that the financial advisor honor their original agreement (which was not in writing), the advisor showed Mike the door.

Mike had a lifetime of experience complaining when things went wrong; this behavior had deteriorated every relationship he had ever had. It's no wonder he was single, and now he was out of a job again.

As he complained to his mother about this latest injustice, it brought back memories of countless similar conversations. Before he had his own stories to complain about, Mike remembered listening to his mother complain about all of the companies she had worked for.

This could have gone on and on, but Mike heard me speak at a conference and was moved by some of my ideas. Within a week, he had hired me as his coach.

As he shared some of his complaints and stories, I noticed they all centered on people who promised him everything and delivered nothing. I told Mike that what he was actually angry about was being abandoned and unloved by his father.

Mike exclaimed that he didn't even know his father, and repeated his stories about how the photocopier sales manager and the financial advisor had promised him everything and delivered nothing.

I told him again, "What you are really angry about is being abandoned and unloved by your father."

"You don't understand!" Mike was starting to get angry. "This is about what those bastards did to me. All they did was take and take and take."

I gave my message again. Mike felt angry about being abandoned and unloved by his father.

This time, Mike looked right into my eyes and repeated with me, "I felt angry and unloved because my father left me."

Tears started to flow. As Mike wept, he felt like a thousand pounds had been lifted from his shoulders. He realized that the sales manager and the financial advisor were just representations of the father that he had never known.

Mike asked how could his father have done this to him and left him all alone. Wasn't he good enough? Didn't his father love him?

We talked about forgiveness and understanding; we all do the best with the resources we've been given. After all, Mike's father's father probably wasn't very kind and loving towards him. He could not give Mike something that he did not have to give.

It was clear that Mike had been avoiding these feelings for years. We talked about how thoughts are real forces, and how we attract whatever we believe. Mike's underlying belief that he's not good enough was continually attracting the circumstances and people to make it real.

I asked him if he was ready and willing to clear his *Unmet Need* for approval and his negative emotions and negative beliefs.

Mike agreed to give it everything that he had.

We went through the process outlined earlier in this book. Mike wrote out his story and did the work to clear his negative emotions.

Next, I showed him how to apply a very similar process to clear his negative beliefs about his father, the sales advisor from the photocopier business and the financial advisor who'd brought him into the industry.

Father

Step 1. – Identify your negative beliefs

Step 1 I believe that I am not good enough

Step 2. – Forgiveness

Step 2   Forgive me for believing that I am not good enough

Step 3. – Create positive beliefs

Step 3   Forgive me for forgetting that I love myself

* * *

Step 1 I believe that my father does not love me

Step 2 Forgive me for believing that my father does not love me

Step 3 Forgive me for forgetting that my father loves me and did his absolute best

* * *

Step 1 I believe that my father hates me

Step 2   Forgive me for believing that my father hates me

Step 3 Forgive me for forgetting that my father loves me and did his absolute best

* * *

Step 1 I believe that my father is a coward

Step 2   Forgive me for believing that my father is a coward

Step 3 Forgive me for forgetting that my father must have had some significant challenges that caused him to leave and he still loves me

Sales manager

Step 1 I believe that nothing I do is good enough

Step 2 Forgive me for believing that nothing I do is good enough

Step 3 Forgive me for forgetting that I did a remarkable job of selling photocopiers and provided excellent service to many happy customers

* * *

Step 1 I believe that the sales manager is a jerk

Step 2 Forgive me for believing that the sales manager is a jerk

Step 3 Forgive me for forgetting that the sales manager was doing the best that he knew how

* * *

Step 1 I believe that the sales manager hated me

Step 2 Forgive me for believing that the sales manager hated me

Step 3 Forgive me for forgetting that the sales manager could not see beyond the rules that he created

Financial advisor

Step 1 I believe that the financial advisor will burn in hell

Step 2 Forgive me for believing that the financial advisor will burn in hell

Step 3 Forgive me for forgetting that the financial advisor had invested a lot of time in his clients and could not let go

* * *

Step 1 I believe that the financial advisor is a liar

Step 2 Forgive me for believing that the financial advisor is a liar

Step 3 Forgive me for forgetting that in his own way, the financial advisor helped me transition to the financial advisor profession

* * *

Step 1 I believe that the financial advisor is a cheat

Step 2 Forgive me for believing that the financial advisor is a cheat

Step 3 Forgive me for forgetting that I worked through the situation and became an excellent financial advisor in the process

When we met up again in a week, Mike shared the work he had done to clear his negative beliefs. Writing the story of how he felt about not having a father was the hardest thing he ever had to do. I suggested he pretend to sit his little boy self down on his knee and put him in charge of the writing. When he did that, "It was as if the negative emotions and negative beliefs were flowing out of my body right onto the page... My negative ego mind did not want me to do this and told me that I could not handle this, but I did it anyway. What I began to realize was that the negative emotions and negative beliefs only got so strong and there was a point where they did not get any stronger and began to melt away. When I was finished, I felt ten years younger, happier and lighter in my body. I also realized that there isn't a negative emotion or negative belief that I can't get rid of in a short period of time."

Step 4. – Clear your emotions and beliefs and then apply your work to your business

To make this process even more powerful, combine your work to clear both your negative emotions and negative beliefs and add in the business applications from The Clear Values Scorecard.

	Financial Survivor	Financial Advisor
1	I lack focus.	I follow a written 5-year vision and business plan.
2	I am not making as much money as I would like.	I am fully satisfied with the amount of money I am making.
3	I have to get myself pumped when I am selling.	I feel naturally excited about my work and I enjoy the selling process.
4	I feel I am not getting enough referrals.	I am getting many great, qualified referrals.
5	I feel that I am working too hard, with too many unqualified or C and D clients.	I am getting many new high-quality clients.
6	I try to serve anyone and everyone.	I have branded my business and I am focused on a niche market.
7	I do too many favors and I sell too many products.	I am focused on profitable products and services.
8	I feel completely overwhelmed, doing things I don't like to do.	I do what I love to do and have a hiring system to delegate everything else.
9	I have a lot of conflict in my business relationships.	I manage my business relationships extremely well.
10	I beat myself up when things don't go right and I have lost my enthusiasm for my business.	I always celebrate my successes and learn from my setbacks. I am achieving my true potential as an advisor.

Examples:

Step 1 I feel angry that I don't have a vision for my business

Step 2 Forgive me for feeling angry that I don't have a vision for my business

Step 3 Forgive me for forgetting I am feeling alive and I can create anything that I choose to

* * *

Step 1 I feel ashamed that I am not making enough money

Step 2 Forgive me for feeling ashamed that I am not making enough money

Step 3 Forgive me for forgetting I am feeling confident, that I have the clients, prospects and skills to achieve my financial goals

* * *

Step 1 I feel bitter that clients don't always purchase the product recommendations that I offer

Step 2 Forgive me for feeling bitter that clients don't always purchase the product recommendations that I offer

Step 3 Forgive me for forgetting I am feeling energetic. I will use this energy to increase the number of product recommendations with the outcome that I will attract my sales goals

* * *

Step 1 I feel dejected that I am not asking for and receiving referrals

Step 2 Forgive me for feeling dejected that I am not asking for and receiving referrals

Step 3 Forgive me for forgetting I am feeling excited because I have the confidence, experience, knowledge and skill to ask for and receive qualified referrals.

After our initial work together to clear his *Unmet Needs*, negative emotions and negative beliefs, Mike was ready to jump in and get things happening for himself at a new firm. "It's a good thing I don't have a written agreement with that other advisor," he realized, "I'll just convert all of my clients over to this new firm and off I go."

But I said, "Not so fast." I wanted to investigate Mike's *Unmet Need* for approval a bit more. While the *Unmet Need* for approval was an asset that caused him to give good service and be well liked by his prospects and customers, he wasn't qualifying or segmenting these clients the way he needed to. Add to that, his *Unmet Need* for approval caused Mike to take rejection very hard.

First, I showed Mike a way to segment his clients so that he could make the best use of his time. We were also laying the foundation for Mike to get referrals.

I asked him to list all of his clients and identify the ones that he really liked and that really liked him. Of those, I asked him to identify the ones with a strong business and family network to draw referrals from. Finally, of those, I asked him to rank them by their amount of assets.

This three-step client segmentation process gave Mike the focus he needed to re-connect with all of his clients.

Now it was time for him to ask for the referrals. I explained that the best time to ask was when you feel like you have added value to your client, when you sense that you have a good connection.

Mike was reluctant to ask for referrals because he had never done it before, so I gave him a script to practice.

Referral Script

I am looking for ways to improve my service to best assist my clients...

To find ways to design my business around people like you, I would really like your help and input by asking for your answers to the following questions.

What do you like best about the work that we do together? (Be ready. Write down the answers to the question.)

Is there one thing that I do for you that you did not expect? (Be ready. Write down the answers to the question.)

How could I improve the way I work with you? (Be ready. Write down the answers the question.)

NOTE: If anything comes up that your client needs from you at this time, commit to do the work, record the information, thank the client, and follow up in one week to confirm that progress is being made.

If no service is required, continue with this script...

Thank you very much for your kind words.

Who can you introduce me to who would appreciate this same kind of service?

IMPORTANT – wait 3-5 second before continuing.

As I told Mike, this is the most important part: When you ask this question, wait three to five seconds, and then say, "Do you know what? When I ask this question, most people don't have a name or two at the tip or their tongue. What I find is when I call them back in seven to ten days, someone always crosses their path who would make a great candidate for a referral. Would it be okay if I called you back? Here is the kind of client that I am looking for.

"By the way, I would like to send a copy of your comments for your approval. That way I can share your comments with prospective clients who are thinking of working with me. I'll get them out to you and follow up in a few days."

After seeing this script, Mike said he could never use it.

- What if I make a mistake?
- What if they think that I am too pushy?
- What if they say no?

I told him, "It sounds like you have some negative beliefs to clear about asking for referrals. I'll see you back here in a week."

We continued to meet on a weekly basis. Moreover, Mike continued to do the necessary work on himself. He went on to create a strong foundation for both his business and personal life, providing consistent service to the many clients that he attracted by referrals.

As I said before, the process to clear your negative emotions and negative beliefs is for your private use. It is not recommended that you share your work with anyone. They may not understand this process and they could take it personally.

If you are tempted to share your work, are you trying to meet a need for approval or worthiness from outside yourself? Is your negative ego saying, "Look how good I am?" Remember, thoughts are real forces and you will attract an outcome based on your *Unmet Need*, negative emotion and negative belief.

Maybe you are not coming from an *Unmet Need*, maybe you just want to share what you are doing because someone else might benefit from hearing it. Noble, yes, but don't do it.

For example, if you were to share this with a loved one:

Step 1 I believe that people only take and take and take

Step 2 Forgive me for believing that people only take and take and take

Step 3 Forgive me for forgetting that I love the work that I do for people and enjoy adding value.

Chances are that all they would hear is that you believe people only take and take and take, and whammo, you have just opened up Pandora's Box. They're bound to take it personally and to react from their negative ego mind.

If you want others to benefit from this process, use the form on the website to send them a complimentary copy of the e-book and leave the work up to them. It is not your job to clear the *Unmet Needs,* negative emotions and negative beliefs of others.

Chapter 11:

Get Clear on Your Vision and Goals

Step 1. - Vision worksheet

If you could wave a magic wand and be looking back on the year from December 31st...

- What would have to have happened for you to be happy with the progress that you have made in the past year?
- What did you accomplish?
- What goals did you set and achieve?
- What made you happy?

Use the following project areas to remind you of all the goals that you could be setting in both your business and personal lives:

Business	Personal
Administration	Auto
Clients	Clothing

Computers, Systems and Technology	Charity
Customer Service	Entertainment
Financial	Family
Marketing	Friends
Planning	Health
Product Development	Hobbies
Production	Home
Sales	Intellectual
Team	Spirituality
Training	Spouse
	Travel

Write your goals down in detail, using the five W's – who, what, where, when and why – but forget about how.

Step 2. - Goals to reach in the next 90 days

Now come back to the present moment. Of all of the goals you imagined you accomplished by the end of the year, which ones would you most like to set for yourself for the next 90 days?

Make sure you select those goals that you really want, not ones you should, could, ought to, or might want. Give some serious thought to setting both your personal and business goals. Also, tap into your feelings. When you have set the right goals for yourself, you should feel excited, a little nervous, ready and willing to go for it.

Sally's story – goals were not enough

Sally is considered to be one of the best advisors in the region. She got her start working within the banking industry and after ten years of experience, decided to go out on her own. That was almost twenty years ago and now, business is booming.

Sally consistently takes a couple of days at the end of every year to redefine her vision and set her 90-day goals. She provides her clients with life insurance, critical illness, disability insurance, group insurance, employee benefits and money products. Her firm's customer service is second to none and she has an assistant specializing in each of the product areas her company sells and services. Customer satisfaction is first and foremost to Sally as she has a perfectionist nature.

I guess you could say that Sally is the rainmaker who brings in all the business, while her team of assistants make sure that the work is processed, crossing all the T's and dotting all the I's.

Business kept flowing in. Sally was well liked and recognized because of her strong community service, being a past president of the local chapters of the Cancer Society, Chamber of Commerce and Rotary.

To eliminate the ups and downs in her moods, Sally did her share of personal development work over the years. She understood that the origin of her *Unmet Need* for perfection was related to her upbringing and the relationship she had with her father and older sister.

When she was growing up, it seemed like a day did not go by that she heard her father say, "Look how good Julie is doing," or, "Look at the way Julie is dressed," or, "Look at the marks that Julie got, you should be able to do much better."

While this seemed like a curse from her child-hood, through deep reflection, Sally came to realize she was perfect just the way she was. She did not need to compete for the love of her father and her father did love her. He simply wanted her to do well because he could see, even at a very young age, that Sally had a lot of determination, focus, drive and people skills.

She saw all of this as a blessing but something still seemed to be missing.

Through the consistent work Sally did every year on her vision, goals and action plan, she was meeting and exceeding her expectations in all areas of both her professional and personal lives. She had a great business, marriage and her health was excellent.

While the firm was flourishing, Sally was beginning to lack the enthusiasm to grow the business and break the illusive 2 million dollars in sales, the mark of a champion in her industry.

No matter how hard she tried, she could not figure out why she was losing the drive she once had. It turned out that her vision, goals and actions were missing a crucial foundation – values.

Chapter 12:

Get Clear on Your Values

Remember, values generate positive feelings and positive beliefs. Values are the DNA of fulfillment. They help you to source your inspiration, get you up in the morning and pull yourself forward. They are the catalyst for the Law of Attraction.

Let's use the goal of asking for referrals as an example.

The values involved might be abundance, attraction, energy and service. The positive emotions are excitement and energy. The positive belief is that clients receive great benefits from the products and services that you offer, and the outcome is many referrals asked for and received.

Clients want to do business with advisors who have energy and passion. That's how it works. It is not about you; it is about the benefits that you can bring to your client and the referral.

Step 1. - Choose your values

Please review the following list of values and circle the ones that speak to you the most:

Accept	Collect	Edify	Give
Accomplish	Command	Educate	Gloriousness
Acquire	Communicate	Elect	Glow
Adept	Community	Elegance	Govern
Awake	Compassion	Embrace	Grace
Adopt	Compel	Emote	Grant
Advance	Compete	Empathize	Greatest
Adventure	Complete	Endeavor	Guide
Affect	Compliment	Endow	Heal
Affirm	Compose	Energize	Hedonistic
Alleviate	Conceive	Engage	Hold
Alter	Confirm	Engineer	Holy
Amplify	Connect	Enhance	Honor
Amuse	Consider	Enlighten	Host
Appreciate	Construct	Enlist	Identify
Arouse	Contact	Enliven	Illuminate
Ascend	Continue	Enroll	Impact
Assemble	Contribute	Entertain	Imagination
Assist	Counsel	Enthuse	Implement
Associate	Create	Evaluate	Improve
Attain	Danger	Excellence	Improvise
Attract	Dare	Excite	Influence
Attractiveness	Decide	Exhilaration	Inform
Augment	Defend	Experiment	Ingenuity
Aware	Delight	Expert	Inspire
Beauty	Deliver	Explain	Instruct
Believe	Demonstrate	Explore	Integrate
Best	Design	Express	Invent
Bestow	Detect	Extend	Involve
Bliss	Devise	Facilitate	Keep
Bond	Devoted	Family	Know
Brighten	Direct	Finance	Labor

Build	Discern	Forgive	Launch
Call	Discover	Foster	Learn
Catalyze	Discuss	Franchise	Link
Cause	Distinguish	Further	Locate
Choose	Distribute	Gamble	Love
Claim	Dream	Gather	Loveliness
Coach	Drive	Generate	Magnificence
Make	Predominate	Resonate	Superiority
Manifest	Preeminence	Respect	Support
Master	Prepare	Respond	Surrender
Mature	Present	Restore	Sustain
Measure	Prevail	Return	Synthesize
Mediate	Primacy	Revise	Take
Minister	Prime	Risk	Taste
Model	Produce	Rule	Teach
Mold	Progress	Sacrifice	Team
Motivate	Promise	Safeguard	Tenderness
Move	Promote	Satisfy	Thrill
Negotiate	Provide	Save	Touch
Nurture	Pursue	Score	Trade
Observe	Quest	See	Translate
Open	Radiance	Sell	Travel
Organize	Realize	Sensation	Triumph
Originality	Receive	Sense	Uncover
Outdo	Reclaim	Sensitive	Understand
Participate	Reduce	Sensual	Unite
Pass	Refine	Serve	Uplift
Passionate	Reflect	Sex	Use
Perceive	Reform	Share	Utilize
Perfect	Regard	Spark	Validate
Perform	Reign	Speak	Value
Persuade	Relate	Speculation	Venture
Plan	Relax	Spiritual	Verbalize
Play	Release	Stand	Volunteer
Pleasure	Religious	Standards	Win
Possess	Rely	Stimulate	Work

Practice	Remember	Strengthen	Worship
Praise	Renew	Summon	Write

Step away from the list for a while and then come back to it for the next step.

When you come back to the list, star (*) the seven values that are the strongest.

Step 2. – Link your values to a positive feeling

Your next step is to link each of your top seven values to a positive feeling. Please refer to the Positive Feelings List in Chapter 8, Step 1.

Step 3. – Link your values to a positive belief

To create your positive belief about each value, affirm that you are meeting your goal and that your negative beliefs are untrue. You must determine what is true instead.

For example, if a negative belief about your writing skills is impacting your goal of publishing a newsletter, transform it to the positive belief that, "My writing skills are getting better and better."

Step 4. – Write your Clear Values Statements

Now, pull it all together and create Clear Values Statements, linking your values, positive feelings and beliefs to the goals you have chosen to accomplish over the next 90 days.

Here are some examples of Clear Values Statements:

- I observe that my value of <u>teaching</u> is being met, therefore I feel <u>excited</u>, resulting in the positive belief that <u>my writing skills are getting better and better and I am adding more and more value to the clients whom I serve.</u>
- I observe that my value of <u>listening</u> is being met, therefore I feel <u>passionate</u>, resulting in the positive belief that <u>my research and presentation skills are getting better and better and I am adding more and more value to my clients every time I offer a proposal.</u>
- I observe that my value of <u>abundance</u> is being met, therefore I feel <u>excited</u>, resulting in the positive belief that <u>I am attracting more worthy and qualified clients through my actions and thoughts.</u>

Write out two to three of these Clear Values Statements for each of your goals, each expressing a different value.

George's story – finding the passion again

Life insurance was George's business but somehow he had lost his passion for it. Too much transactional paperwork, relating to the money side of his business, bogged him down. It wasn't always this way.

Back in the eighties and nineties, once the details of the initial insurance sale were recorded, that was it. All he had to do was take care of the client relationship.

To him, all of the hassles started in the late nineties when banks decided to get into the insurance business as well. Everyone now felt they had to offer both insurance and money products, like mutual funds, to compete with the banks. George had to track a lot more information related to the transactions taking care of his clients' investments.

He was tired of both the life insurance business and this new "money business." He found himself at the stage where he either had to hire an assistant for the money business or sell it. In fact, it had been so long since he focused on life insurance sales, he felt like he had forgotten how.

He recalled a coaching exercise a fellow salesperson had shared with him many years earlier. He'd been feeling low about his performance, and this other salesperson suggested that George had forgotten about the value he was adding to his clients.

The salesperson had attended one of my workshops and learned the above process to get clear on your values. He taught George how to do it.

George identified his top seven values, chose a list of positive feelings and linked them together into Clear Values Statements. Though he didn't feel better overnight, in a few days he felt the cloud of negativity pass. He started to regain his enthusiasm.

Years later, when he thought back to this process, it did not take George all that long to realize he had been wallowing in self-pity along with the paperwork.

George decided to apply the same exercise to his current struggles with the insurance business. Here's a sample of one of his Clear Values Statements:

- I observe that my value of accomplishment is being met, therefore I feel energized, resulting in the positive belief that life insurance is an excellent investment for families to create a positive foundation as they move forward to build their lives, knowing that they are well protected.

With the focus on expressing this value and belief, he set up meetings with his best clients to address the fact that their life insurance was severely underfunded.

He told them a brief story and then asked them a question, because if he didn't no one else would.

On the evening news the week before, there was a picture of a family in their pajamas standing in front of their burned out house. The dad stood there in dress shoes and his workout gear. The reporter gave instructions for where to send donations, and explained that some kind soul had lent them enough to stay at a local motel for a week.

George ended with, "The last thing the TV announcer said before the end of the news clip... they didn't have insurance."

In the case of one particular couple George spoke to, the father of the family did a lot of flying for business and he was underinsured by at least a million dollars. This was determined after taking into consideration the fact that the couple still had a mortgage, a high-interest line of credit and a son they were putting through university.

Because of George's beliefs about insurance and the value that he was now committed to express, he went on to ask them the question that most financial advisors fail to ask, because they are afraid to. He asked them, specifically the husband, "What if you have a heart attack or stroke?"

He went on to describe two different scenarios:

Scenario A is you have remained underinsured. What happens to the mortgage, to the kid's plans for university and to the lifestyle that you have gotten used to as a family? How will you deal with these worries at the same time you are trying to heal?

Scenario B is you are covered by critical illness and have life insurance in place. As you are sitting in that hospital bed, surrounded by your family, you can focus on healing, knowing that you did the right thing for your family by investing in insurance.

George further pointed out that we all find the money for things that we think we want. For the price of a latte a day, it is possible to invest in the extra insurance to take responsibility for your family. And then, he closed with, "May I have your permission to start the paperwork for the insurance?"

Chapter 13:
Stay Clear with Practice

Step 1. – The choice of practice

It was Friday at 4:05pm, November 26, 2007 and I was waiting for my last coaching call of the week. And oh, what a week.

It started on Sunday at 4:45am, getting ready for a flight to London, Ontario to speak at Pro-Seminars first thing Monday morning. I flew back the same day and coached from Tuesday to Friday.

On that Monday afternoon, I began to practice by celebrating being so blessed to have an incredible amount of space during the 9 to 10 hours of travel time each way. My travel time includes a one-hour drive to the airport, time in the airport lounge, time between flights and cab rides to the hotel. Where else in your life do you have 20 hours of solitude to get clear? I chose to celebrate and not to hang up on comments I heard that day, like:

"How do you do it? I could never do that. Oh, you are going to feel it on Tuesday. I could never sit still that long. It would drive me crazy."

It is about practice. I practice bringing business development and client files with me on the flight so I am making 101% use of my time. I am rarely sitting idle except when I am taking a meditation break or when I am finished with my work.

Funny, idle is synonymous with lazy, vain, unoccupied and unemployed. Idle also sounds like idol – didn't someone once say it is forbidden to worship false idols?

"How do you do it? I could never do that. Oh, you are going to feel it on Tuesday. I could never sit still that long. It would drive me crazy."

How do I do it? I choose to practice. Some of the other ways I practice and clear regularly are to:

- Journal. Writing connects me instantly with feeling because my body is engaged in the process as well as my mind. As I see what I'm writing, I'm hearing it internally and paying more attention.
- Mediate. I take time for meditation and affirming infinite energy first thing in the morning. I take breaks during the day to recharge my body and mind with infinite energy.
- Exercise. Vigorous, cardio exercise two to three times per week.

Step 2. – Give thanks

The practice of giving thanks helps to create and stay connected with inspiration and helps you stay connected to your values, positive feelings and positive beliefs.

Henri Nouwen, the late Catholic psychologist and spiritual guide, wrote: *"To be grateful for the good things that happen in our life is easy, but to be grateful for all of our lives - the good as well as the bad, the moments of joy as well as the moments of sorrow, the successes as well as the failures, the rewards as well as the rejections - that requires spiritual hard work."*

The ability to feel the whole range of negative emotions and positive feelings allows us to amplify our positive feelings overall. This is why it is so important to clear your *Unmet Needs*, negative emotions and negative beliefs. Rather than *deny*, we *amplify* and through this, we *magnify* the ability to attract what we want and release and complete what we do not want.

Actors have the ability to feel and portray this range of negative emotions and positive feelings. That's why the great ones are paid so much. Actors are a conduit to the emotions and feelings that our negative ego mind shuts down, and watching them allows us to access those feelings.

A common method for practicing gratitude is to write a daily or weekly gratitude list. I'll share two examples, one focused more on business projects and one focused more on personal projects.

On Friday, November 26, 2007, I wrote this:

It has been a great week because of the following:

- Practiced my daily meditation first thing in the day and practiced during the day to NOT get sucked into the high drama that some of my clients are creating in their negative ego mind and to more importantly ignite infinite energy and to provide my clients with the same
- Personal journaling reexamining the patterns that I can easily get hooked into when I do not do my practice, and more importantly to affirm my positive practice
- Managed and tracked all files and information in a system, keeping me from being over-whelmed and making it easy to manage and prioritize information
- Reading
- Completed 4 power rides on my bicycle
- I made a list of inspirational movies that I will purchase on DVD to have available versus TV
- Had a conversation with my mother and she is in good spirits
- Ordered new shirts to replace the ones that have shrunk and that I have killed with the odd pen to make sure that all areas of my pre-sentation are 101%
- Our business is in flow as we have a consis-tent number of clients and it is now just about maintaining the process. Yes, there are some big projects to complete like the book, group coaching, upgrading the clear your roadblocks e-book and web site... the key is we have a strong foundation
- Experienced the benefits of adding 2 ½ hours per coaching day of non-coaching time

- A business development loan repayment is in sight and the money will be then available for another investment
- Pre-prepared for my coaching calls with clients a day in advance
- Celebrated a number of miracle outcomes with my clients - it is a joy to work with those that really do the work and to experience significant changes in a short period of time
- Clients continue to hire us for special projects that include; hiring an assistant, coaching junior advisors, one-on-one business planning retreat and a clear your roadblocks one on one retreats - we only have one open day for client work between now and the end of January. Keep in mind we have time for personal time, management, product development and clients.
- Laura filled our clients schedule up to March 2008
- Organized the filming of the 8:00 am presentation we are doing for Pro-Seminars on Monday, November 26th
- Examined the automation of our follow up to the attendees of our public speaking
- Worked on our 2008 speaking schedule
- Improved our One Sheet for our public speaking marketing
- Being more aware of Advocis Chapters that we can contact for 2008 speaking. Contacted Peter Lantos of The Elite Advisor to have a conversation about how we can best help each other
- Speaking leads are being followed up
- Created an Elevator Speech Assignment

- Thought of a few product names for our new group coaching product
- Improved my power point by reducing the presentation down from 110 slides to 50 slides
- An invitation to write for The Advocis FORUM Magazine again
- Started an article called weathering the potential economic emotional storm
- New clients are coming into the business via the internet, past clients coming back, referrals and speaking. I am quite pleased to say that a client came in through the one-on-one coaching pages that explain our coaching process on our web site. This was after and through a meditation where I asked that we continue to attract new clients both easily and effortlessly. We are on-track with our sales forecasts.
- Kim Black our IT expert has completed a number of tweaks on the web site
- Simon Parsons our computer expert introduced me to the Fly Fusion Pentop Computer
- Scheduled December so that I can enjoy the holidays and get four days of writing in at the same time

And, on October 5, 2007, I wrote this:

Wishing all of you a Happy Canadian Thanksgiving - Monday, October 8th.

I'm calling this an Open Blog because I will be adding my List Of What To Give Thanks For over the course of today and the Thanksgiving Weekend.

I'm thankful for:

- Family - I will call my mother Irene over the course of the weekend and talk with her on the phone and I give thanks that she is in good health and well taken care off.
- Laura's mom Helen will be coming to stay with us for the weekend to celebrate Thanksgiving and I am so looking forward to family time as we have many blessings to give thanks for.

6:30am, Monday, October 8, 2007

- Family and Friends - Laura's beautiful table setting just before Helen, Laura and I sat down for Thanksgiving Dinner on Sunday, October 7th with our friends Charline and Allan.
- Health - May we always be Happy and Healthy.

Thanksgiving Long Weekend - I'm thankful that I have taken the Saturday and Sunday and I'm on my way to making Monday three days in a row of non-business activity.

1. getting lots of extra sleep
2. puttering around the house getting it winter ready - storm doors and weather-stripping
3. meditation
4. journaling
5. reading
6. who knows, we may even go to a movie

As I re-read these gratitude lists, above all, I am so thankful that I am working with my clients who have taken the steps/are taking the steps to clear their roadblocks to success. They are attracting business effortlessly and easily and therefore, we both feel appreciative, energized, excited, happy and looking forward to the future.

My other regular gratitude practices are to:

- Tell Laura that I love her
- Affirm "forgive, forgiven, forgotten"
- Perform an act of kindness
- Thank my clients for the opportunity to be of service

The more I practice these things, the more I attract them. I am like a sunflower following the flow of the sun's radiance. As I do, I grow stronger and stronger.

What happens when I don't practice? I fall into these old patterns, some of which may sound familiar to you:

1. Feeling afraid - based on the *Unmet Need* for safety
2. Complaining and judging that nothing is good enough - based on the *Unmet Need* for worthiness
3. Going in circles or going from one thing to the next with judgment and no sense of appreciation - based on the *Unmet Need* for approval
4. Making lists to keep track of it all - based on the *Unmet Need* for control
5. Setting expectations that are too high - based on the *Unmet Need* for recognition
6. Not prioritizing and seeing every task as critical, which keeps me going in circles - based on the

Unmet Need for safety

7. Getting angry because it appears that not enough is being accomplished - based on the *Unmet Need* for worthiness
8. Feeling worn out
9. Feeling like a victim and telling a story to justify my negative experience; "You don't know how bad my life is because I have experienced; a, b, c, etc."
10. Blaming
11. Attracting crisis

By reviewing the following project areas and writing down what you are thankful for today, you can start your own practice right now.

As Eckhart Tolle would say, "the present is perfect," so you could start with the gratitude that you have the time, resources and willingness to read this book and do this work.

If your negative ego mind is chiming in with negative beliefs, you now know what to do. You need to wake up and clear your *Unmet Needs*, negative emotions and negative beliefs.

Project areas

Business	Personal
Administration	Auto
Clients	Clothing
Computers, Systems and Technology	Charity
Customer Service	Entertainment

Financial	Family
Marketing	Friends
Planning	Health
Product Development	Hobbies
Production	Home
Sales	Intellectual
Team	Spirituality
Training	Spouse
	Travel

Step 3. - *Your real wake up call*

You are familiar with the first wake up call of the day. You are rousing from sleep and immediately your negative ego mind starts talking to you:

- What do I have to do today?
- Whom do I have to see today?
- How will I earn extra money today?
- Whom do I have to impress today?
- What conflict do I have to deal with today?

Then the next level of worry and negativity:

- Am I safe?
- Am I good enough?
- What do I have to do next?
- Where do I have to go next?
- What do I have to buy next?
- Who is looking at me?
- What do people think of me?
- How does what I have compare to what others have?

Enough.

Stop.

Shut up, negative ego mind.

It is time for your second wake up call.

The second wake up call is when you, your higher self wakes up.

When your higher self awakens and lets go of these other thoughts, of all thoughts, you just experience the moment and think, "Hmmmm..."

As I work during the day, it is important that I stop every so often to ask, "Am I awake"? It is important that I give my mind a rest from thinking, or I can easily become consumed by the thought addiction of the negative ego mind.

Thoughts related to thought addiction are based upon *Unmet Needs*, which trigger negative emotions and negative beliefs. It stands to reason that any resulting ideas about vision, goals, projects and actions are doomed to failure because of where their foundation lies.

I want everything I do to be based upon conscious being. You can achieve conscious being by taking time between tasks to wake up and practice not thinking. For some of you, this means to know God or to know another spiritual force. This practice reminds me of my values, positive feelings and positive beliefs, because all those things are related to conscious being and that spiritual force.

Step 4. - Waking up with Eastern and Western psychology

As you observe yourself waking up in the morning:

Be aware and mindful. Ask, "How do I feel?" If the answer is positive, breathe it in. If the answer is negative, have compassion for how you feel. Following Eastern psychology, simply stay in the moment with the negative emotions and breathe. The idea is to be awake and mindful and be familiar with and aware of your emotions exactly as they are in the moment. It's like offering unconditional love to an old friend.

Do not buy into your negative ego mind's negative beliefs and stories about not having enough time, that you are too busy, that you have to do this and that. Stay awake and mindful; stay in the moment. Breathe through the negative emotions. The more you do, the more the pain will subside. You will be able to tap into your passion like never before.

Following Western psychology, ask what situations the negative emotions remind you of. Now, you can clear your *Unmet Needs*, negative emotions and negative beliefs as we've practiced in this book. This is a fantastic system for quickly getting clear of any emotions that may be weighing you down, so you can wake up right.

Step 5. – Practice

As simple as the clear your *Unmet Needs* process looks, I can't say enough about using it. You have heard the expression that it takes 21 days to break a bad habit. Why not adopt the affirmation that it takes 21 days to create a brand-new habit? Use this process to clear your *Unmet Needs* for 21 consecutive days.

Create the habit of meeting these key needs for approval, control, recognition, safety and worthiness on a subconscious level. The result will not be an earth-shattering event, like the high you might have felt coming out of a motivational seminar. Rather, you will notice a subtle and calming change come over you. You will gain a sense of inner strength. This is not the same as being hyped up because you think you now have power over your emotions or beliefs. Power is an *Unmet Need*. If you need power over something then it has power over you.

Repeat this process to clear your *Unmet Needs*:

I observe my *Unmet Need* for safety is being cleared whenever I _____ and therefore I feel _____.

Look back to the Positive Feelings List in Chapter 8, Step 1.

The next time you get into a negative emotion or negative belief; record it and what triggered it. Spend some time with yourself and your journal to clear your negative emotions and negative beliefs. Give yourself 45 to 90 minutes.

In the early stages of this work, make an agreement to sit down with your journal and ask yourself, "What do I have to clear?" I promise you, even though you may not think you have something to clear, something will come bubbling up.

It could be a situation like:

- An argument with a colleague
- A client rejecting a product offer
- A prospect saying no

On the other hand, it could be emotions you are noticing, such as:

- Frustrated about the fact that you said yes to doing a favor and now you resent the extra time you have to put in
- Overwhelmed with too much to do
- Remorseful about poor sales results for the month
- Tired out

Step 6. – Meditation and prayer

> *Prayer is when you talk to God; meditation is when you listen to God.*
> Author unknown

I respect your creed, religion and beliefs, whatever they are. My own experience, before I fell away from the Catholic Church, was that instead of praying to God, my negative ego mind was too busy judging the people that were trying to practice their faith.

> *When there is no understanding, there is judgment. When there is judgment, there can be no understanding. Judgment and no understanding are what cause you to beat yourself up.*

Seek first to understand yourself and judge no one. Don't forget, whenever you point a finger at someone, there are three fingers pointing back at you.

How you pray and meditate is your business, I only suggest that you do it.

Step 7. – The "secret" to the Law of Attraction

The Secret popularized the idea of the Law of Attraction (originally from the groundbreaking work by Esther and Jerry Hicks).

> *It is inevitable that you will always be moving toward something. So, why not be moving toward something pleasurable? Find thoughts that feel good. "You can't cease to vibrate, and Law of Attraction will not stop responding to the vibration that you are offering."*
> Esther and Jerry Hicks

The following are affirmations I was inspired to write and practice after reading Michael Losier's book, Law of Attraction:

- I have decided to attract and meet people that will receive value from product XYZ. Therefore, I feel energized, optimistic, enthusiastic, confident and happy.
- I am in the process of attracting and meeting people that will receive value from product XYZ. Therefore, I feel energized, optimistic, enthusiastic, confident and happy.

- A lot can happen in the months of April and May to attract and meet people that will receive value from product XYZ. Therefore, I feel energized, optimistic, enthusiastic, confident and happy.
- God is allowing me to attract and meet people that will receive value from product XYZ. Therefore, I feel energized, optimistic, enthusiastic, confident and happy.

The *Unmet Needs Disease* is an overgrowth of negative emotions and beliefs that leads to ineffective behavior and an inability to conceive or carry out a strong vision and plan. This, in turn, inhibits the fulfillment of dreams and stunts financial, emotional and personal growth.

You can make the choice to use the Law of Attraction in a positive way. To clear your *Unmet Needs*, negative emotions and negative beliefs and make way for your values, positive feelings and positive beliefs.

Congratulations on coming this far.

The choice is yours.

The Gift

You were born perfect and were meant to deliver a special gift to humankind. A gift that is unique to you and that only you can give.

In order to fulfill your destiny, you must choose the road less travelled and remove the roadblocks to your success. Only you can do this, and only if you clear your *Unmet Needs*, negative emotions and negative beliefs.

The road is not an easy one, and may appear to have many obstacles that you cannot overcome.

Just when you think that you are through your roadblocks, you may be tested by some challenging emotions. You may feel:

- Unfocused and can't see your vision
- Fear about money
- Exhausted about the lack of sales
- Rejected when you forget to clear before asking for referrals
- Angry because some clients are never satisfied
- Confused about which niche market
- Unclear about products
- Overwhelmed with too much to do
- Frustrated with your relationships
- Self abused

You will come to realize that these emotions are actually a blessing. They remind you it is time to wake up, that life is a journey, not a destination. Part of the journey is to learn to appreciate these feelings, because it is by working through them that you will magnify your inner strength.

As you take charge of the wheel and clear your way though the roadblocks of *Unmet Needs*, negative emotions and negative beliefs, know in your heart that you will breakthrough to the other side.

You will know peace of mind and consistent success, as you notice that money is becoming easier to attract. You will look forward to your sales calls, because of your new found confidence from within. You will notice that your clients volunteer referrals without you even asking. You will have more time because you are working only with the clients you enjoy the most. You have become an expert in a niche market and are the recognized expert in your area. Your team supports you and your clients every step of the way with a "can do" attitude.

Your love of self has become real and you devote time to continually improve your personal and professional development. You are in excellent health and you travel with your family and friends.

Through the routine practice of giving thanks and staying awake, through meditation and prayer and reminding yourself of your values, positive feelings and positive beliefs, you are magnifying your special gift and adding value to all whom you serve. And through this, all of your own dreams continue to come true.

Simon Reilly

September, 2008

Afterword

You CAN make a difference.

The Starfish Story, Loren Eisley

One day, a man was walking along the beach when he noticed a boy picking something up and gently throwing it into the ocean.

Approaching the boy, he asked, "What are you doing?"

The youth replied, "Throwing starfish back into the ocean. The surf is up and the tide is going out. If I don't throw them back, they'll die."

"Son," the man said, "don't you realize there are miles and miles of beach and hundreds of starfish? You can't make a difference!"

After listening politely, the boy bent down, picked up another starfish, and threw it back into the surf.

Then, smiling at the man, he said... "I made a difference for that one."

You too can make a difference, starting right now. I invite you to send free downloadable copies of the first seven chapters of the **Curing the Unmet Needs Disease** book to your associates and friends.

Here is an example of an introductory email that you can send.

Dear (Name of associate/friend),

*I've just completed reading the Curing the Unmet Needs Disease book and I'm following through on Leading Advisor's invitation to send you a free downloadable copy of the first seven chapters of the **Curing the Unmet Needs Disease**.*

As a fellow Financial Advisor, I know how hard you are working. All of us are spinning our wheels and striving hard to succeed in a challenging economy.

I learned so much from Curing the Unmet Needs Disease, practical information written especially for Financial Advisors. It is helping me look at my practice in a whole new light and make some significant positive changes.

Since this book helped me so much, I thought you'd appreciate a heads up on this new resource.

Best of all, it is free. Check it out at <u>www.leadingadvisor. com/thecure</u>

Thanks, (Your name)

Thank you for making a difference in the world by sharing this book and helping another financial advisor. Your actions today will have a ripple effect on everyone whose lives they touch.

To Work Individually with Simon

Coaching – Sustainable Support for Successful Advisors

A positive prognosis

The 3-step Clear Your Roadblocks Program is designed to clear the way to follow the 10-step Leading Advisor Coaching Program. Here are some of the objective business and personal results that our clients have created from a typical quarter:

- Asked a non productive senior manager to leave
- Bought out a partner
- Built and/or upgraded the web site
- Completed an audit
- Completed the vision and goals for a five year plan
- Created two new world-class product ideas
- Eliminated miscommunications
- Exceeded a sales campaign goal by 25% (the goal was the highest ever to begin with)
- Healed from an operation
- Hired a new business manager

- Hired a new full-time assistant and associate agent
- Implemented a brand-new marketing plan
- Listed their home
- Made an offer on a new office
- Made number 2 in the office
- Made number 3 in the office
- On track to be the first one in the region to break 1 million in sales volume
- Opened a $1 million case
- Produced a new e-newsletter
- Provided an in-office team building workshop that joined the team together in a brand-new way and ignited the team's passion like never before
- Purchased a brand-new car
- Purchased a brand-new SUV
- Purchased and installed a new computer system
- Purchased a new house
- Purchased critical illness and life insurance
- Purchased new suits, shirts, ties and shoes
- Reached $3.5 million in sales
- Re-financed the business
- Relationship reignited and brought to a whole new level
- Re-negotiated a contract with a number one supplier
- Re-negotiated a takeover bid for the company
- Resolved conflicts
- Started and completed sales campaign
- Traveled to and attended a conference
- Traveled to and attended a study group
- Went to Europe
- Year end completed with sales 45% over forecast

Who is coaching you?

Ron James is a Canadian comedian, and we saw him on a Canadian Broadcasting Corporation TV special in March 2007. He joked that traditionalists are out there saving every dime, while these boomers are spending every cent of it. They're off to the spa with a bottle of Pinot in one hand and a life coach in the other. "A life coach," he said, "What the heck is a life coach?" When he heard that it's someone you pay and they give you advice, he said, "Isn't that what friends are for? I'll give you some advice - you drink too much and you are an asshole!"

All kidding aside, is there anyone in your personal or business life qualified to guide you through the process of curing your *Unmet Needs* and generating a successful financial advisor practice?

Consider hiring a specialist, someone who can be neutral, detached and non-judgmental. Someone who:

- Is fully trained and experienced on how to clear your roadblocks to building a successful and sustainable business
- Wants only the best for you
- Holds what you say in confidence
- Will not judge you
- Gives you the mandatory time to work "on" your business versus "in" it
- Provides insight, inspiration, perspective and new ideas
- Provides immediate solutions and action plans
- Will give you tough love

- Will "call you" on it when you are not being honest with yourself
- Holds you accountable so you take action

What is the cost of staying sick?

While we go through the fallout of the Sub-Prime Mortgage Crisis, consider how time flies.

We saw the tenth-worst stock market crash in history after 9/11 and it has been almost a decade since the dot com bust.

The Barings Bank Crisis was back in 1995. Were you in business yet when that happened?

So, while you are being bombarded by negative press coming at you at an accelerated rate, pinch yourself. These cycles can come and go. After all, the end could have been back in the 1980's, when Bunker Hunt devastated the silver market, when interest rates were at an all-time high of 21% and the US fell into the Savings and Loan crisis.

As we look back on these historic events that shaped our industry, think back on the early decisions that shaped the current reality of your financial advisor practice.

Were you plagued by the *Unmet Needs Disease*?

Or...

Did you start out with a vision for the future and a strong business plan?

Did you have excellent financial controls that allowed you to have peace of mind?

Did your vision, business plan and financial controls allow you to attract the kinds of clients you enjoy working with and provide you with many qualified referrals?

If so, I am sure you have built up a thriving and successful practice and that you are living the life of your dreams. Though I wonder what attracted you to this book if that is the case.

More than likely, if you have gotten this far in the book it is because you identify with the *Unmet Needs Disease,* and you see how its negative emotions and negative beliefs have contributed to the following issues in your life:

- Lack of focus
- Not enough money coming in
- Loss of motivation
- Failure to ask for referrals
- Too many small clients and small products
- Administrative "busy work" that takes all your time
- Conflict and disputes with clients, partners, management, associates and staff
- Beating yourself up

Now, look forward: where will you be five or ten years from now if you continue to work without the systems that you so desperately need?

If you enjoyed working through the exercises in this book but would like to go deeper into this process, consider working with Leading Advisor in a coaching relationship.

Make a difference for yourself

Before we begin working with our clients with the 10-step Leading Advisor Coaching Program, our clients start with the 3-step Clear Your Roadblocks Program.

The 3 steps of the Clear Your Roadblocks Program are:

1. Clear Your *Unmet Needs*
2. Clear Your negative emotions
3. Clear Your negative beliefs

We provide the 3-step Clear Your Roadblocks Program via:

- One-on-One Tele-Coaching
- Group Tele-Coaching

The 3-step Clear Your Roadblocks Program includes:

- Values and behaviors assessment – completed and delivered online
- Values and behaviors assessment debriefing – 1 hour telephone debriefing
- Assignments and systems to identify and meet your *Unmet Needs*, negative emotions and negative beliefs
- Assignments and systems to identify and integrate your values, positive feelings and positive beliefs into your vision, business and marketing plan
- Bi-monthly one-hour coaching calls for 2 months
- Weekly goal tracking software
- 24/7 email and/or telephone access
- Access to our Knowledge Bureau

The first step of the 3-step Clear Your Roadblocks Program uses a scientific approach that starts with values and behaviors assessments.

As we've learned in this book, values are what inspire you and impel you to take action towards your goals. While working with hundreds and hundreds of clients through their assessments, Leading Advisor has benchmarked the values and behaviors of today's most successful financial advisors. We further identified six key values, and we will see how these specific values are expressed in your assessment.

Your behaviors are the methods and actions you take toward attaining your goals. As we've discussed, behaviors are either an expression of your values, or they are a manifestation of your *Unmet Needs* and their accompanying negative emotions and negative beliefs, which conflict with or overshadow your values. At the end of the day, that leaves you with conflict, inconsistency, lack of motivation and even worse, an unfulfilled business and personal life.

Through values and behaviors assessments, the 3-step Clear Your Roadblocks Program helps our clients to understand and implement the values and behaviors that are required to renew and maintain sustainable and consistent success.

If you want to maintain, build or turn your business around, the 3-step Clear Your Roadblocks Program is the only sustainable system for building a strong foundation for your business to stand on.

The Clear Your Roadblocks Program creates a foundation to build a strong and sustainable business and work towards achieving these benchmark criteria from The Clear Values Scorecard:

1. I follow a written 5-year vision and business plan and I always have enough time.
2. I am fully satisfied with the amount of money I am making.
3. I feel naturally excited about my work and I enjoy the selling process.
4. I am getting many great, qualified referrals
5. I am getting many new high-quality clients.
6. I have branded my business and I am focused on a niche market.
7. I am focused on profitable products and services.
8. I do what I love to do and have a hiring system to delegate everything else.
9. I manage my business relationships extremely well.
10. I always celebrate my successes, learn from my setbacks and I am achieving my true potential as an advisor.

The 3-step Clear Your Roadblocks Program leads directly to the 10-step Leading Advisor Coaching Program:

1. Create a vision for the future and develop a business plan
2. Implement excellent financial controls and make more money
3. Refine your sales skills
4. Attract many qualified referrals
5. Assist high-quality clients and delegate your C and D clients

6. Become a recognized expert and create a unique brand focused on an affluent niche
7. Focus on profitable and specialized products and services
8. Recruit, lead and delegate to a championship support team
9. Create harmony in all business relationships and deliver amazing customer service
10. Celebrate your success and achieve your true potential

For more information about coaching, public speaking presentations, retreats and workshops, please contact Laura Reilly at lreilly@leadingadvisor.com or go to www.leadingadvisor.com/.

Thank you for taking the time to invest in your success.